This Stretch of the River

Craig Howe and Kim TallBear, Editors

Cover photo by
George Brennaman and Lydia Whirlwind Soldier

Printed in the United States of America

PINE HILL PRESS
4000 West 57th Street
Sioux Falls, SD 57106

OAK LAKE WRITERS' SOCIETY

This book is a publication of the Oak Lake Writers' Society, a state-wide organization of Dakota, Lakota, and Nakota writers. The Society is an outgrowth of the summer retreats for aspiring tribal writers that have taken place at South Dakota State University's Oak Lake Field Station since 1993. The primary goal of the Society is to contribute to the strengthening and preservation of Dakota, Lakota, and Nakota cultures through the development of culture-based writings.

ACKNOWLEDGEMENTS

We are very appreciative of the funding support of the Brookings Reconciliation Council and the individual donor contribution of Harry Peacock, as well as the writers' retreat funding support of the South Dakota Humanities Council and South Dakota State University while this book was being written. We are also very appreciative of the administrative assistance of First Bank and Trust of Brookings and its president, Van Fishback.

Finally, this and all other projects of the Oak Lake Writers come to fruition in no small part because of the diligent commitment and wise guidance of Charles Woodard, co-founder of the Oak Lake Writers' Society and Professor of English at South Dakota State University. Dr. Woodard consistently offers editorial guidance to individual writers, good stories and humor, and moral and fundraising support. He is also largely responsible for organizing the annual summer retreats at Oak Lake. We are deeply appreciative of his contributions and his belief in the worthiness of our group and our various projects.

TABLE OF CONTENTS

INTRODUCTION

This Stretch of the River is a project initiated by the Oak Lake Writers' Society in response to the bicentennial observances of the Lewis and Clark Corps of Discovery expedition. It was conceived at the South Dakota State University Field Station along the western shore of Oak Lake and in the back room of the Hendricks, Minnesota café in the summer of 2002 during the course of the Society's annual retreat. Thus, it appropriately has roots in both South Dakota and Minnesota, the two states with the largest populations of Dakotas, Nakotas, and Lakotas, the tribal names of people collectively and incorrectly labeled "Sioux," who knew themselves as Oceti Sakowin, the Seven Council Fires.

The impetus for *This Stretch of the River* was a desire to present Oceti Sakowin perspectives and responses to the Lewis and Clark expedition and its bicentennial commemoration. We wished to write back, now two hundred years later, to the expedition journalists—Meriwether Lewis, William Clark, John Ordway, Patrick Gass, and Joseph Whitehouse—and to the historians and chroniclers of the expedition. But perhaps more importantly, we wished to address our neighbors and fellow citizens, and the "big muddy" itself, the Missouri River.

The Lewis and Clark expedition looms large in the history of the United States. It was a monumental undertaking that understandably is acknowledged for its geographic scope and intellectual and political aspirations. But too often it has been imagined and described as a virtuous journey conducted by heroic figures of impeccable character. The words that those individuals committed to paper, then, are too often treated like sacred texts which are unquestionably true and therefore not open to critical analysis or contradictory positions. The focus is predominately on the two men, Meriwether Lewis and William Clark, and on the expedition as a great travel adventure across an "unknown" continent. The expedition is seen from this perspective as the leading edge of the plow of Manifest Destiny.

As such, the Lewis and Clark expedition is viewed with pride by many Americans. It is a feel-good story about a small, determined group of diverse individuals who, by their wits and their hard work, traversed the breadth of this country and returned to tell about it in their own words. Theirs was a remarkable feat, but it was also a harbinger of dramatic changes for the peoples, places, plants and animals along their route. In the wake of their keelboat and canoes, devastating processes were set in motion with effects still rippling today. These are the perhaps unintended—and usually unexamined—consequences of the expedition.

This Stretch of the River seeks to present alternative perspectives to the mainstream narratives of the expedition and its consequences. It positions the Missouri River in a central role. *This Stretch of the River* begins with the Missouri River itself, with the river foregrounded as a powerful living entity. Only then does the expedition come into the picture, both in its broad scope and in its particular time in Oceti Sakowin territory. The ramifications of the expedition are then critically reviewed and personal reminiscences of the river are shared. The focus is on this stretch of what appears on maps as the Missouri River, but is called Mnisose in the Lakota language.

Method and Ethics: Working Together as Tribal Writers

This anthology includes poetry, fiction, memoir, history, and literary criticism, with a range of political opinions and differently seasoned voices. We range in age and social roles from young adulthood to being grandmothers and grandfathers. A few of us are students and others are teachers at public or tribal schools, tribal colleges, or universities. Some of us are new to publishing and others are not so new. What brings us together is our orientation as Lakota, Dakota, and Nakota writers; we all write from within Indian Country some or all of the time.

Before moving into the featured pieces, we want to address several issues of method and ethics endemic to our group that have come to the fore in putting together this collection. We do not refer to a formal system of ethics, but rather to the idea that because the Oak Lake Writers are organized as a group of tribal writers based in South Dakota, we are compelled to consider our topics and our voices as more than simply individual projects. Our tribal-family entanglements (sometimes unfortunately!) are not left behind when we enter the calmer space of our annual retreat at Oak Lake, near Astoria, South Dakota. The retreat is a productive space in which we share our writing, in which we generate ideas for projects such as this book, and in which we discuss tribal histories, politics, and the ups and downs of writing amidst busy lives. Though we each take our own work to the retreats, we are all guided in our subject matter, our tone, and our methods by tribal social and cultural standards and pressures. Our work is shaped by those standards and pressures at home, and tribal dynamics—ways of being and working—also shape our interactions and our work together.

In producing this anthology, two important lessons emerged. First, we learned that the individually-authored text generates special predicaments for tribal writers. Conscious of being accountable to our communities and families in the things that we write about and, perhaps more importantly, in the things that we do not write about, interesting conflicts can arise as we produce texts under our individual names. That is not to say that we are not inspired or ambitious to develop as individual writers, or that we never cross the taboo lines where our families and tribal communities are concerned. We may write something that some others think should remain private. Or we might render a historical, political, or personal interpretation that others simply disagree with. But those pressures and standards are ever present for the tribal writer. Indeed, being conscious of and receptive to their guiding forces, if not always submissive to them, is a central ethic for each of us.

Yet the majority society view of the practice of writing is that it is as an individual accomplishment, a matter of individual (if not legal) freedom of expression and the presentation of the individual voice. Certainly, tribal writers are subject to that view of creativity. Also, like most authors, most of us do not submit readily to critiques and editing. We are wary of our individual voices being stifled or our meanings altered. In addition, living in the contemporary world, most of us have suffered a good deal of hostility to our cultural and familial practices and to our tribal histories. Important to our being within the tribe, to thinking of ourselves as Dakotas living among other Dakota, for example, is continuously referencing our jointly remembered history, even as we encounter dominant knowledge and institutions in which there is little room for our interpretations. Therefore, it is safe to say that as tribal writers we are especially leery of censorship, even amongst ourselves. Subjecting our individually-authored texts to the assessing eyes of one another can sometimes feel like being personally judged. And it might also feel like a devaluation of those personal/family/tribal stories that are so crucial to being Dakota, or Nakota, or Lakota. Yet the very act of producing a "book" usually implies something cohesive and whole with a definitive beginning and end. Editors conjoin disparate pieces into something intelligible for the reader. So it is a project unavoidably fraught with contradiction.

Out of uneasy moments, however, we learned additional important lessons. One of the final pieces in this anthology, the dialogue-essay, first occurred to us (the editors) as a process and text that might help us draw together the individual pieces. During the dialogue, we asked the writers to center the river as an entity in and of itself, to tell us about Mnisose— what it means and what it has meant to tribal life. But in addition to the compelling histories shared by the writers about the river, profound insights into tribal ways of knowing and working together came to the fore, both during the dialogue and in later conversations about how to transcribe and edit it.

The dialogue is very much a multi-authored piece, although the editors eliminated many of the imprecisions and fillers of speech (i.e. the "ums" and the "ers" and sometimes repetitive or meandering passages).

After initial transcription, the writers reviewed their words, in some cases deleting and/or adding text in order to clarify or fill out their descriptions, analyses, and assertions. The purpose of the dialogue was to create a conversation which would culminate our multi-authored yet tribal text appropriately, emphasizing the variety of our experiences and the many tones of our voices. The dialogue foregrounds our differences as well as the histories that bind us together. The dialogue—like the Oak Lake organization— helped us to tend our relationships, which have their ups and downs, and to reaffirm important cultural knowledge among ourselves. At the same time, the dialogue provided a high level of control by contributing writers and predictably it engendered less writer objection to editorial management than did our suggested edits to individually-authored pieces. Thus, the dialogue has served both our needs to have our individual voices heard and that ethic of joint tribal remembering—that sharing of histories that ensures their longevity.

In addition, our joint remembering prompted each of us to dig deeper into memory and into our analyses of the effects of changes to the river on our cultural and familial practices. Accounts emerged in conversation that reached a level of complexity not as easily achieved in our individual pieces. The dialogue also includes insightful accounts of the way that daily and sacred practices (so tightly wound together) were intimately related to Mnisose's particular ecosystem prior to the damming of the river that began in the 1940s. Disagreements or questions between us also prompted additional critical analysis. In summary, the dialogue enabled us, as a group of Dakota, Lakota, and Nakota writers, to collaboratively produce work in a way that upheld certain tribal standards of decorum.

The Works

We enter *This Stretch of the River* by way of Lydia Whirlwind Soldier's poem, "Mnisose." It presents a deep personal relationship to the river and focuses our attention on the river's inherent and ongoing power. "My Beloved River" by Gladys Hawk continues in that vein. In it she shares memories of her early years growing up along the Grand River, a tributary to the Missouri, demonstrating very expressively what a resource such memories can be. In "The Beginning of Sorrows," Kathryn Akipa tells childhood stories of life near the river—"slice of life" stories that are both happy and tragic. She also describes the devastation for the community members of Lower Brule when their village was flooded by the construction of the Big Bend and Fort Randall dams. But Akipa does not focus only on the tragedy of the river project for Native people. She also describes the aftereffects of the flood in a way that conveys the substance of the crucially important daily relationship between Native people and the river. In the end, hers is a story that reaffirms that on-going relationship.

"The Renaming of a Nation," another composition by Lydia Whirlwind Soldier, links these personal and poetic stories of the river to the Lewis and Clark expedition. In a wonderfully undulating sequence of prose and poetry, she retells the history of the entire expedition. "The Missing Voices," by Elden Lawrence, argues that the expedition was a historical continuation of the centuries-long legacy of invasion that originated in the Old World with the Crusades. Craig Howe, in "Feasting on Lewis and Clark," offers an alternative to the mainstream historical narratives of the encounters between the expedition and the Lakotas. Kim TallBear extends this critical examination in her review-essay of Stephen F. Ambrose's Undaunted Courage, a historical treatment of the expedition that focuses on Meriwether Lewis' role. She examines Ambrose's fascination with Lewis and the expedition and asks what it says about American politics that Ambrose's particular brand of history and storytelling is so appealing.

Elizabeth Cook-Lynn's "Assigning Meaning to the Lewis and Clark Adventure and the Western Story" also addresses the nationalist politics of writing American history, including writing about Lewis and Clark. But she also goes beyond the Corps of Discovery to focus on the centrality of the Journal, the Photo and the Fictional Narrative as crucial documentation for what she terms "colonial historiography." Charmaine White Face illuminates the ramifications of the colonialism that conceived the expedition in "Where Are They?" an essay that questions the fundamental premise that colonialism is benevolent.

Zion Zetina, in his poem "Native Reaction," captures the energy and spontaneity of slam poetry as he focuses on Lewis and Clark. Intended for performance, his voice is edgy and direct. The poem helped win Zetina the slam poetry competition at the 2004 South Dakota Festival of Books. Joel Waters, in "A Nickle for Your Thoughts," shifts the gaze directly to you, the reader, and encourages you to reflect on the ramifications of the expedition and its commemoration, using the common commemorative device of a newly-minted coin to address the obvious ironies of American history. Gabrielle Tateyuskanskan's "Isanti River Journey" describes the spiritual and historical centrality of the Minnesota and Mississippi Rivers to Dakota people. But her prose poem is also a tribute to rivers more broadly and to their life-giving power for tribal peoples.

"Reflections on Mnisose after Lewis and Clark" is a dialogue between six members of the Oak Lake Writers' Society. Taped at Java, South Dakota in February of 2005, the dialogue centers the Missouri River as a living actor in the years between the Corps of Discovery journey and its bicentennial commemoration. The writers talk about their personal relationships with Mnisose as well as their families' and their peoples' relationships with the river. They describe the profound disruption to communities and cultural practices caused when the US Army Corps of Engineers flooded and dammed Mnisose.

Kim TallBear's poem "Solitary," written for and about her maternal grandmother, depicts a formative childhood memory of life lived alongside another river, the Big Sioux, in eastern South Dakota. The Big Sioux landscape and her grandmother's relationship with that river are TallBear's reference points even as she writes in a tropical landscape on the opposite side of the globe.

And in "Mni Wiconi," Lydia Whirlwind Soldier returns us full circle back to the Missouri River as an everlasting and living entity. It was here before Lewis and Clark, and before the Lakota, the Dakota, and the Nakota. It will remain after humans are gone. *This Stretch of the River* concludes with "River Power" by Lanniko Lee. Lee's poem, with its ultimately optimistic language of love, power, comedy, adventure, and dreams, affirms Lakota, Nakota, and Dakota relationships with Mnisose, and all of the rivers of our tribal landscapes.

Craig Howe, Martin, South Dakota
Kim TallBear, Sisseton, South Dakota and Tempe, Arizona
December 2005

Mnisose

Lydia Whirlwind Soldier

Mnisose in simple terms
means muddy water
I wonder how this great river
expresses itself now that it is not free
my friend, Roselie, a Miniconju Lakota
lived on a houseboat with her grandfather,
when she came home to heal her
boarding school wounds
life linked to the river was hard
but free and happy
they fished, hunted
on sandbars they played
in inlets they swam away
from floating turtle mothers
when the sun dropped below the hills,
they ate scarred catfish on fire-lit shores
they heard ghost stories
pumas scream and coyotes howl
they stared into the fallen stars night
and frogs croaked their courting songs,
life then teemed with whooping cranes and eagles
the shores were heavy with trees and game,
that was when the river was free
but that was long ago, before
wounds were left on the land, before
nearly every stream was molded in
concrete and civilized
elders wept when a Hidatsa chief signed
away the river, again on the bluffs
elders wept, calling out name after name
villages vanished, life on the river
quietly slipped into the darkness
of rising water

Now, life grows stagnant
large bodies of mirrored water stand,
whitecaps flash in the wind with no place to go
runoff from plowed fields and feedlots
gather into cesspools until gates open
to water streams below
in my mind's shadows Mnisose shines
with the morning star, and hope flares with the
bursting seeds of prairie flowers
I know nothing chokes the spirit
of the damned river
nothing chokes the powerful purpose
of this silent creation—Mnisose

My Beloved River
Gladys Hawk

There are now only patches of a lake that once was so full that one could barely see tree tops. A few spindly pieces of wood stick out of the water, remnants of what were once majestic cottonwood, oak, elm, and other kinds of trees native to the river. It is now also easy to see familiar landmarks that I remember as a young girl, growing up in this quiet and serene environment. Sadly, the great Oahe Lake is drying up.

I can clearly remember the fall leaves turning the surrounding landscape of the river into a beautiful variety of colors, hues of orange, yellow and brown mixed with some green. In the fall my parents would gather wood for colder weather. Fallen tree branches were first piled here and there to be hauled home later and my father would cut notches into a few green ash and oak trees to be felled later. My mom would find a few strands of wild grapes wrapped around some of the branches. Wild grapes are grayish, and they blended with the plum and wild rose bushes, making them difficult to find at times. She would make grape jelly that didn't last very long, not with five hungry men in the house.

The Grand River was home to many animals as well, and we, the original dwellers of the area, can appreciate this source of sustenance. Game and fish were plentiful. The one hunted animal that still stands out in my mind is a whitetail buck with huge antlers. He was prized game, according to my brothers.

This also brings to my memory times when the boys went "spotting" for deer at night. In those days, there were no restrictions or laws on what, when or where to hunt. The boys would drive out at night in my dad's pickup truck; two seated in the cab, the driver and the controller of the spotlight, and two riding in the back, standing above the cab of the truck with their guns at the ready. The terrain was familiar to them, so they usually had good luck. They would bring home two or three deer on a good hunt. I can still see them as they skinned and butchered the deer under our arbor, which also served as a resting place for travelers who would stop for a refreshing drink of water from the barrels that stood in the shade. My mother would serve whatever kind of food she had on hand to the travelers, who were often relatives.

I also remember the boys hunting on horseback. One time, they decided to make a "deer drive" from west to east along the river. An old riverbed that used to be the main channel of the river but was changed to curtail flooding in later years always had water in it and served as a habitat for many creatures, including birds, beavers, and turtles. A blind had been built so that my father could sit and wait for the deer. It took one to two hours to make the drive. As the boys on their horses chased the deer toward the area of the blind, they heard a gunshot, followed by another that echoed up and down the river. They were elated as they raced to the blind, thinking that the old man had gotten a deer or two. My father, an old World War I veteran, was a sharpshooter. However, the boys arrived just in time to see the old hunter fishing a huge beaver out of the water. The disappointed hunters must have said a few cuss words. But they carried the beaver home and that evening, we had a good supper of beaver soup.

From the skins of animals, my brothers usually received homemade "choppers" for Christmas. These were mittens that served the purpose of keeping hands warm as they buzzed logs and chopped wood for our stoves.

The long hot lazy days of summer always found me outdoors. I was the only girl in our family, but I most enjoyed helping with chores outside or riding my horse along the river and visiting neighbors. My mother understood my lack of interest in domestic duties. However, I learned these duties in great detail when I attended a mission school, under strict conditions, of course!

We had many horses, and each summer there were always the yearlings and two-year-olds that had to be "broke" to be either saddle or wagon-trained. There was a wide sand bar near our home which was a perfect place to break horses, and my brothers had a great time getting the horses used to bits, bridles, and saddles. Once in a while, they would put me on a horse and turn it loose and I would try desperately to fit myself to the rhythms of the horse as it twisted and turned. Sometimes the horses we were breaking would run into the willows, kicking high to try to throw riders, but the boys were very adept at riding these young horses. I don't think my mother knew I was actually involved with the breaking of horses. We were mostly able to avoid injuries because if we were thrown, we landed in deep sand.

The sand bar had a pretty good growth of willows on it, which were useful for drying the towels and blankets that Mother and I washed in the river. I remember the time my mother dropped a bar of Fels Naptha soap in the water. The swift current carried it away in a matter of seconds. The water was so clear that it was easy to see the soap as I scrambled to retrieve it. I would help my mother wring the blankets and towels. They smelled so clean. Then we would throw the washed towels and blankets over the willows to dry in the hot sun. One could say that we polluted the water by doing our laundry in it, but it seemed the natural thing to do during those times. The river always stayed fresh and clear because it flowed continuously.

The Grand River would rise after a good rain and occasionally, my dad would find a huge log that had drifted down from the west that was useful to us. He would make a chopping block or cut short sections to be used as chairs. Especially after a rain, I would collect various sizes of clamshells. I remember the faint rainbow colors on the insides of those shells.

I recall especially a very moonlit night when my boyfriend and I sat along the banks of the river in my car and saw the reflection of the moon sparkling and dancing on the water as it mirrored back to us. He had traveled on horseback from further down the river to meet me at our river crossing. That night we heard Patti Page sing "Allegheny Moon" on the car radio. The August moon seemed to hang heavily in the sky as it made its way through the night. We were so young. We sat and talked about our experiences and our dreams for the future.

He came from a somewhat affluent family in Indian country. They raised cattle, and were very successful. My family was more into the church community and didn't possess many material goods. I had big dreams of becoming a musician, not knowing too much about it, and he wanted to become a mechanic, as I recall.

Our romantic interlude was a once-in-a-lifetime experience, but one that I will always treasure. The river provided the backdrop of this romantic scene, with its occasional cadence of a ripple from the rushing water as it washed ashore and the smell of the willows that permeated the still air of the quiet night. The hooting of an owl, the horse stomping its leg, and the call of a bullfrog could also be heard occasionally as we nestled against each other, both of us nearly falling asleep as we listened to the popular songs of the time.

Finally it was time to part. The waxen moon seemed to also bid us a final farewell. After a brief hug, and a kiss, we said goodbye. I watched as he rode off across the river until he disappeared from sight. The memory of this night is magical for me because of the river.

The Beginning of Sorrows
Kathryn Akipa

The celebrated journey of two American heroes across what is now known as the western United States stirs the red, white and blue blood of patriotism in the hearts of most Americans. Since 2004, the celebration of the 200th anniversary of the Lewis and Clark Corps of Discovery Expedition has been foremost in the collective consciousness of many Americans. Celebrations all along the now-historic Missouri River route of Captains Meriwether Lewis and William Clark have been taking place in their honor. From local media blitzes intended to entice tourists, to humorous skits and plays of reenactment, to the marketing of memorabilia, reproductions and trinkets, to festive parades and noble speeches, America has been commemorating the voyage of the Corps of Discovery and its crew.

However, even though some of the North Dakota tribes may welcome and participate in the celebration, some of us to the south do not feel the same about this portion of American history. For the Ikce Wicasta (Common Man), or "Sioux," as most know us, Lewis and Clark and the Corps of Discovery signaled the beginning of the end of our great culture as it once existed on the Northern Plains. It was "the beginning of sorrows" initiated by these strangers on our sacred waterway, the Mnisose. Now, I have my small story to tell, a story which is part of that long and drawn-out process initiated by Lewis and Clark.

From the beginning, it is said, Lewis and Clark were in search of a western water route to the Pacific Ocean. Commissioned by Thomas Jefferson for this task, Lewis and Clark and their crew were prepared to be the first ones to set foot in places where "civilized" men had never trod, although they knew when they left their camp at Wood River in May of 1804 that they would encounter tribes along the route. There were dozens of tribes already living along the Missouri River, but they assumed that they were the first "civilized" men in these parts.

This is not surprising. Our Native civilizations have never been recognized in the context of American expansionism. In the minds of colonialist Americans, we tribal people remain the eternal "savages." If we had not had this identity in the American psyche, then we would have had to have been dealt with at a different level. Of course, recognizing and dealing with us as "civilized" human beings would have definitely flown in the face of "Manifest Destiny." The horrific Native American history that has followed in the wake of the passage of Lewis and Clark's keelboat on the Missouri beginning in 1804 has raised a question in the minds of many Native people: Since their sailing two centuries ago, if the treatment that we Native people have received by the "civilized" people of America isn't "savage," then...what is?

Historical Sorrows

In the late 1950s and into the early 1960s, I lived in the Indian village of Lower Brule, South Dakota on the beautiful western bank of the Missouri River. By now, the Great Sioux Nation had fought wars with the US government over the land which we called home. As a hunting and gathering people, our traditional economic grounds ranged from southern Manitoba and Saskatchewan in what is now Canada to the north, to the Grand Teton Mountains of the Rockies in the west, to the North Platte River and beyond in modern-day Nebraska to the south, and eastward, to the Mississippi River and beyond. The heart of these places and what we believe is the heart of the earth is our sacred Paha Sapa, the Black Hills. Having lived and moved in this manner of seasonal hunting and gathering for untold generations, we Lakota, Nakota and Dakota truly have held aboriginal title to this area.

For the "savage" acts of protecting our hunting grounds to continue to be able to feed our families, we have endured holocausts at the hands of the "civilized" Americans, including massacres of unarmed Lakota elders, men, women and children under the white flags of truce and the forced removal and imprisonment of Dakota and Nakota women and children (several from whom I descend). The forced walk of these ancestors of mine, from western Minnesota to Fort Snelling in modern-day Minneapolis, ended in their imprisonment in the concentration camp there. We will never forget their blood which stains the Minnesota earth under its modern highways and their forced walk into concentration camp oblivion. To this day, we walk for them and wokiksuye (have memorial) for them and pray for our own healing of multigenerational trauma and grief in those very places where they suffered.

My great-grandmother, whose English name was Emma Ortley Crawford, was a four-year-old child on this forced removal of 1,700 Ikce Wicasta. Her mother was killed at the beginning of the walk, and as a four-year-old child, she endured being urinated on and had settlers' feces and their rotting slop and boiling water thrown upon her as she passed through the white settlers' towns of southern Minnesota. She healed from those burns as a child, but the scars of hatred she endured for the crime of being Dakota remained an open wound in her psyche for the rest of her days. These events were a short six and a half decades after the famed voyage of Lewis and Clark.

In the spring of 1862, after treaty signings in which the Dakota people ceded the better part of southern Minnesota and the US government promised to provide annuities to the Eastern bands of Dakota (Sisseton, Wahpeton, Wahpekute and Mdewakanton) whose homelands were in question, the government utterly failed to live up to its promises. The government forced the Dakota to stay in one place and not follow the hunt. It seems that any "unauthorized" movement of any band of the Sioux people made the government wary and overly-anxious. From May to August, none of the promised annuities had been given by the agents. They kept putting off the Dakota leaders and akicita (warriors) who came to inquire about the status of the annuities at the Yellow Medicine and Redwood agencies.

At this time, there was also great discontent between the Dakotas and the traders who had four posts in the area. Andrew Myrick, a shrewd trader who built a store at Redwood Agency, extended credit, as did three other traders, to the local Dakotas based on money to be paid to them by the government for the lands involved in the Traverse des Sioux Treaty. When the payments were not made, Myrick decided to deny further credit. In response to the Indians' desperate condition, he said: "If they are hungry, let them eat grass!" By August, under the order not to hunt, the Eastern Dakota were starving. The elders were failing for lack of food, nursing mothers could not produce milk for their babies and the young men had grown angry with the failure of the government to keep its end of the bargain.

Tensions were increasing between the whites and the Eastern Dakota. A group of young warriors tried to rally everyone they could to destroy the agencies and all those who represented the government. The white settlers of Minnesota seemed to be a blight on Dakota land. The best solution appeared to be to get rid of all the whites, even those Dakota who had white blood. The leaders were initially reluctant to pursue this route, because they had smoked on the agreement in Pipe ceremonies. The Dakota understood that one does not tell lies around the Pipe. After much prodding, however, Little Crow finally agreed to lead the rebellion, and this gave courage to the young, angry akicita. They attacked the agency at Redwood and the surrounding white communities. Four days later, trader Andrew Myrick was found dead on the prairie, with grass stuffed in his mouth.

After the Outbreak of 1862 in Minnesota, over 300 of our men were scheduled to be hanged. To save face, Lincoln, who was fighting a war with the South over the abolition of the slavery of Negroes, commuted the sentences of all but 38 Dakota men. Thankfully, my great-great grandfather, Maza Koyag Inajin (He Who Stands Clothed In Iron), legally escaped those gallows of Mankato. Instead of being released, however, he was imprisoned. In the spring, when the ice broke on the Mississippi, he and other Dakotas who had survived the winter in the concentration camp at Ft. Snelling were barged down the river to Ft. Davenport, Iowa, where he spent five years in prison.

Not many decades after the voyage of Lewis and Clark, the Great Sioux Nation was the target of systematic attempts at total annihilation of our culture and power. These acts were ordered by the US Congress of the "civilized" people, to be perpetrated with "earnest vindictiveness" against our people. The buffalo herds were the basis of our economy, culture and religion. The "civilized" US government knew it and therefore proceeded to destroy the buffalo in order to place the Sioux people and other Plains tribes in positions of utter reliance on the government and its so-called provisions. I believe that we American Indians were also the first to endure biological warfare waged by the

United States government. Since there were no new buffalo robes with which to warm our babies in winter, some of the provisions of the "civilized people" in Washington, DC came in the form of smallpox-infested blankets. Smallpox was a disease not known to the American continents before Columbus. Bogus congressional acts followed, approving the illegal taking and occupying of our lands, and the raping and plundering of our sacred Unci Maka (Mother Earth) for the gold that lay inside the glittering mountain streams of Paha Sapa.

By this time, the US government had, according to its Treaty of 1868, "granted" recognized title of the Black Hills to the Great Sioux Nation. However, because gold was "discovered" in 1874 there, the government of the "civilized" people passed an act in 1877 that allowed them to confiscate our land. This spurious act was in direct violation of the fifth amendment of the Constitution of the United States of "civilized" America. After our defeat of the US Calvary and the death of its military hero Custer in June of 1876, and because we, the "savage" Sioux, had pointed out that they had violated their own highest law of the land regarding their lack of respect for the treaty, the government put us into a starvation period. The annuities from the agents were deliberately stopped.

This act of 1877 further prevented the Sioux from filing any claims for the reckoning of treaty violations until 1920. Surely, the "civilized" Americans hoped that those "savage" warriors of old would be dead by then, their descendents "civilized," and the issue of the Black Hills forgotten. But we, the descendants of those ancient protectors whose precious blood was spilled, will never forget! To this day the sacred Black Hills remain occupied and disputed lands.

Multigenerational Sorrows

One of the saddest of the sorrows we have passed through as Ikce Wicasta in the "civilized" world is that of the boarding school period that followed the institution of the reservations. The majority of us alive today are survivors of that period, or know someone who is. It began in the late 1800s and continued well into the 20th century. This period was characterized by the forced removal of Native children from their homes into boarding schools, some of them governmental and some missionary. The plan was to capture the "savage" children, put them into schools far away, and begin to eradicate every remnant of Native culture, language and identity in them.

My maternal grandmother, Wanbdiwin (Eagle Woman), was born in 1896, orphaned in 1897 and raised by her loving grandparents, who tried to hide her from the agents on their rural allotment land. Much to the dismay of her grandparents, she was discovered at age nine, taken and forced to start first grade at Wahpeton Indian School, a militaristic government boarding facility in southeastern North Dakota. The children were taught English and the basics of Euro-American education. The boys were taught to tend fields and farm animals, and the girls were taught to clean and do laundry. Wanbdiwin stayed there for eight long years, learning to be a submissive Indian in what was now the white man's world. These cultural impositions, 100 years after Lewis and Clark's trip on the Missouri, were still part of the continuum of American progress on the frontier. As Native people, we suffered personal lose, family grief, and cultural destruction after the Voyage of Discovery.

My mother, Wanske (Fourth Born Daughter), was taken with her sisters and others in 1931 at the age of five to mission school 200 plus miles from her maternal home. Some in America have justifiably complained about riding "at the back of the bus," but even that would have been better than what she had to experience. My mother and the other children, ages four to nine, were herded into the back of an open cattle truck like livestock. She rode there halfway across the state exposed to the elements. At dawn in the chill of the early morning air when they were taken, she and the others shivered as they cried. They could not have known whether they shook because of the coolness of the damp, late summer air or because of their violent weeping. In the afternoon, when the sun shone relentlessly down, her baby's skin was scorched; and if it had rained, she would have had no choice but to endure that too.

Attempting to comfort the little ones were the older girls, all of eight and nine years old. Winona, First Born Daughter, and Wanbdi Ahdiwin, Returned By Eagles Woman, hugged and tried to hush the uncontrollable crying of the younger ones. In their pitiful attempts at mothering, Winona and Wanbdi Ahdiwin huddled the children together, and eventually they all fell asleep from exhaustion as they bumped along in the back of the open truck. When it got dark, never having been this far from home before, they were comforted by the sight of familiar constellations in the prairie night sky. These Dakota children knew well the star stories that pertained to the constellations they saw. Though surprised, it made them glad to see that the stars had followed them and looked down upon them as they neared their destination.

Not knowing a word of English, Wanske entered Stephan Mission School, built not far from the eastern bank of the mighty Missouri River. Stephan was a Catholic mission run by German nuns of the Benedictine Order, not far from Ft. Thompson, South Dakota. The beauty of the bright and shining ribbons of sparkling currents, racing along the tops of Mnisose's wide waters on those crisp, fall days, could not dull the overwhelming feelings of disorientation, deep grief and wrenching loneliness felt by my mother and other Indian children at the mission. She was one of nine children, and never had a hand been raised to my mother by her family in her training. Never had she been called names to shame or humiliate her. She had always, especially as a small child, been treated with respect. But now, at Stephan Mission School, over the next several years, life would be drastically different from the life that had been left so far behind. Little Fourth Born Daughter would face corporal punishment, psychological abuse, starvation, humiliation, isolation and confinement by the "holy nuns" of the "civilized" people. This type of treatment of children was not acceptable in Dakota culture and was looked upon as foreign to our philosophy.

In cultural shock, Fourth Born Daughter's first confusing experience at the mission was that of having her hair chopped to just beneath her ears. In her way of understanding, this should have meant that someone close to her had died and this was her mark of mourning; a sign of profound grief. So, the nun's cutting of my mother's hair was ironically appropriate—unwittingly symbolizing the death of her way of life as it was before her arrival to the mission. The next day, in the dining hall, she was surprised and puzzled to see the multitude of children who, like her, appeared to be grieving.

Fourth Born Daughter survived many mistreatments at the mission school. She had her mouth blistered with lye soap for speaking Dakota, the only language she knew. She survived beatings to her knuckles and face with the brass sides of rulers. One night after wetting her bed, she endured being stripped naked, thrown into the showers and left in the dark with no towel. Humiliated beyond her understanding, she was confined there, naked, until the next day. Sobbing and shivering, she shrank into a fetal curl. Finally, sleep came to her, alone in the dark on the bare concrete floor, the coldness of which was rivaled only by the heart of the gray-faced nun who had put her there. The children soon learned that this place of the "civilized" people was not a place of nurturing, kindness and understanding; rather, it was often a place of terror, bewilderment and survival.

A particularly tragic scene haunted the souls of the children during that period at the mission. There were two little boys from Lower Brule, their Native village situated not far across the river. It was common practice for the tribal peoples of Lower Brule and Crow Creek to cross the river on the ice in winter to visit each other. To get to Lower Brule by road would have involved going clear to Chamberlain and all the way around Reliance, involving many miles of travel. The little brothers, ten and seven, were fighting tremendous homesickness and decided that once the river froze, they would run away and get back home to Lower Brule.

Sometime in November, when the older brother had decided that the river must be frozen by then, the boys set out to run away from the mission school. Unbeknownst to them, looming miles away in the west, was a typical South Dakota blizzard. Not far into their clandestine trek, it began to snow and the northern winds commenced to howl against their small bodies. Visibility had become nil and the underdressed little boys could find nothing but a fence post behind which to seek shelter from the storm. They sat huddled together, clutching each other for the only bit of warmth that seemed to exist on the open prairie that night. No one knows for sure at exactly what time, but the merciful hand of death touched these two diminutive human beings, who had preferred to risk death rather than to stay in the school of the "civilized" world.

In the spring, when the snows began to thaw, a local rancher was out checking to see what winter had done to his fences. About three miles from the Stephan Indian Mission, the rancher encountered a gruesome spectacle: the decaying bodies of Newman and his younger brother. Suspecting that the boys had come from Stephan, the rancher went to the school and notified the head priest. The priest went out to identify the bodies.

He promptly got assistance from the nuns and filed all the children out to the site. With total disregard for the sacred and for funerary customs of Indian people, the "holy" man of the "civilized" Catholics forced every child (some of whom were siblings and other relatives of the boys) to look upon their decomposing bodies. The birds of spring had eaten out their eyes and bones stuck out in various places amidst the rotting flesh. The macabre moment was frozen in time in Fourth Born Daughter's mind. Not wanting to look, but being ordered to do so, she glimpsed her deceased schoolmates' remains, noting wisps of hair being moved by the wind and the tattered strips of their clothing lightly fluttering in unison under the bright sunshine of spring. As the children filed by, the priest kept repeating: "This is what happens to bad children who run away."

Personal Sorrows

My formal schooling, first through third grades, was at the Lower Brule Day School, a large wooden building with tall windows built around the turn of the last century during the era of the attempted "civilizing" of my people. Amongst my fellow Sioux students of the Kul Wicasa band of Lakota, we spoke Dakota, Lakota and English on the playground and in the buses. We used English and sometimes Dakota in the classes. Two of our three teachers were Dakota women; one was my mother, the other my aunt. The male instructor and principal was African American, the only Wasicu Hasapa (fat taker with black skin) that many of us had met until then.

Our lives in this little community that spread near the shores of the great Mnisose centered around many new and old elements. "The school" was one of the newer elements. Ball games were held there, as well as dances for the young people, plays for the parents and community, and holiday feeds and celebrations when each child got a Christmas present, even if there were to be none at home. We once used the gym as a huge funeral parlor when we lost eight members of a family who burned to death in the small wooden government housing. The houses were old, unpainted, poorly-made and poorly-wired. It had been bound to happen someday, and it finally had.

The fire broke out in the Goodlow home after the last day of school in the spring. The entire community, so stricken with grief at the immense loss in our little village, pulled together to support the family and one another. There was a child lost in just about every grade except mine. I was in third grade and so was Lonny. He slept on the couch on the front porch that night because the early summer heat was beginning to make life uncomfortable in that small rural place without air conditioning. He was the only one who survived. Lonny's grandmother, Mrs. Crazy Bull, was the cook at the school, and our neighbor the second house around the west side of "the square."

There were no paved streets in "Brulie;" however, we used to play and ride our bikes all over the village. After a rain, the kids who had bikes would look for big mud puddles when they dried, because the fine dust and the gumbo clay would mix together to make hard, smooth, but cracked surfaces. We used to pretend these were our sidewalks like in our Dick and Jane books at school, and would take turns riding over and over them until they broke back up into fine dust again.

On Saturdays, when our chores were done, we would each get a quarter, which seemed like a good amount of money back then. My brother and I would ride down to "the store," where all our rural, school-kid fantasies of shopping were fulfilled. The store was a small one-room structure with benches out front. Inside, there were old-fashioned wood and glass cases to the left, and an old potbelly woodstove to the right with benches and wood chairs situated around it for socializing. Underneath, there were several old rusty coffee cans that served as ashtrays for the men who used to smoke there. The walls were lined with small shelves, some bending in the middles, stocked with all sorts of canned goods. Toward the back were bigger tables for larger items like cloth and outdoor equipment supplies. The floors were creaky wood, lined in worn-off linoleum with occasional nail heads poking through.

Of course, we would immediately gravitate to the penny candy counter, where a seven-year-old felt rich with 25 cents in hand. Our hearts were filled with anticipation as we picked our ten different pieces of candy from a dazzling array of small wrapped taffies, hard candies, and Bazooka Bubble gum and got our standard greasy bag of barbecue potato chips and a seven-ounce bottle of Coke from the red cooler. Sometimes, our mother would send an extra dime for a box of Crackerjacks, her special Saturday treat.

We would walk out of the store, back into the bright sunshine, trying to balance a bottle of pop, an open bag of chips and a kid-sized paper bag with goodies as we rode our bikes away from the store. Rarely did we make it all the way back home with any candy. Our friends would be at different points along the way and would have to see what was in our penny candy bags and would take their pick. We all took turns taking drinks, oblivious to anything called "germs." I didn't mind, as long as I could stash at least half a bubble gum in my front jeans pocket for later.

As a twentieth-century Indian, I had many dramatic childhood experiences in Lower Brule on the banks of the Missouri. I learned how to read and write there, and I had my first fight with my friend Judy. I lost my first tooth there. I learned how to ride bike from my older cousins John and Jim. When I was eight, my mother taught me how to drive her big, chrome-laden pink and white

1958 Oldsmobile on the Spring road, down near the river. We learned how to fight prairie fires. My brother and I got our first pair of cowboy boots when we lived in Brulie. In our minds, they were the toughest boots ever made.

One payday, after we got back from "town" 40 miles away, we ran to show our friends our new turquoise and black boots. We told everyone that the man at the western store in Chamberlain had told us that these boots were so tough, that we could even kill rattlesnakes with them! We all walked along the western edge of Brulie northward toward the river after that, chewing the sweet ends of foxtails and throwing rocks. As fate would have it, the boys found a small rattlesnake coming out of the weeds, and of course, it was now our automatic duty to take on the rattlesnake.

Mom had warned us about the river. Everyone seemed to have a deep and abiding respect for the power and greatness of Mnisose. It was not a place where we were allowed to play. At the river near Lower Brule, there were no swimming beaches and the current was swift.

One summer day, my brother, his older friend Ronnie (who was sort of keeping an eye on us) and I found ourselves down by the river. We were throwing sticks in and having "boat" races with them. All three of us knew we shouldn't have been there, but with no big person around, we continued.

After a while, one of my cohorts got the brilliant idea of using one of my yellow rubber thongs as a boat, just to see if rubber really floats. Reluctantly, I let my flip flop become the object of their experiment. And as many scientists find out, by trial and error, not all experiments go as planned. Ronnie and Russ launched my yellow thong into the water, initially controlling it with long sticks. Much to their delight, it floated as it swirled, spinning into a small current. Then, as it spun out of the current, it was swept way out of reach of our riverbank laboratory. Russ, thinking, "Oh NO! Mom will spank me if we lose my sister's flip flop!" jumped straight into the river to rescue it. Ronnie hollered at him as the current was sweeping my little brother away. Then Ronnie began to run alongside the steep bank, trying to follow Russ as his little head bobbed up and down, in and out of sight in the big river. There was terror in Ronnie's voice as he yelled to Russ. I couldn't really understand why, as I tried to keep up, avoiding sharp rocks and sticks with one bare foot. I kept thinking that he would just turn around and swim back.

By now, Ronnie was shouting at me to keep up and was trying to find a stick big enough to pull my brother back with. In the meantime, Russ kept going under and was being thrown into violent underwater somersaults. He was beginning to swallow river water as he was being plunged in and out. At one point, he opened his eyes to see which way was up and all he could see was brown. Save for the strange muffled sound of the rushing water filling his ears, Russ could not hear us hollering frantically from the banks. This seemed to go on forever, and Russ began to think he was going to die.

All of a sudden, miraculously, Russ felt a great thump as his little body slammed into a junked car mostly submerged near the banks of the rushing river. The old car body had caught up in a fallen tree. Ronnie began to yell with hope in his voice to his elementary school buddy. Then Russ's head finally came up and we dragged him to shore, exhausted and coughing.

Despite trials and tragedies, I have many wonderful memories of that part of my childhood there on the banks of the Missouri River. Perhaps those experiences are partly responsible for the deep affection that my family has for Old Brulie. Governmental attitudes toward the education of Indian children were changing somewhat by then. Although corporal punishment was still allowed, other abusive ways had begun to diminish. Government attitudes toward the land, however, had not. Federal agencies still looked at our ancestral homelands as objectives to be taken, controlled and altered. The land of the Kul Wicasta Sicangu was a casualty of this attitude in that era that I witnessed. With total disregard for the Native people, their community and history there, the government plan was to submerge the land there and relocate the village, all in the mighty name of progress.

In 1961, after learning of Lower Brule's fate, my mother requested a transfer to teach at the Sac and Fox Day School in Tama, Iowa. This news to me was a double blow, because we had just found out that our beloved village of Brulie was scheduled to be "drowned" in a project of the Army Corps of Engineers. This news rent the hearts of the old people, because many were too poor or infirm to see to it that the bones of their grandfathers and relatives would not be disrespected nor forgotten. Our ancestors are never forgotten, because "our lands are where our dead lie buried," as Crazy Horse said, according to oral tradition.

As a result, communal worry and depression gripped the people in those years. Everyone talked about the impending flood: the men in the council chambers, the grandmothers making quilts in their sewing circles, the employees of the school, and even the children playing in the square. At the store, our only formal place of commerce in Brulie, the old men stood around the wood stove, or sat on nearby benches, smoking and agreeing about the callousness of this absurd plan. People felt that life would never be the same again. Their countless memories of generations past, and mine as well, would be buried beneath tons of the chilly waters of the Missouri River Project. A small Native village on the banks of the Missouri River would not matter in the onslaught of American "progress." The US Army Corps of Engineers, a faceless, heartless, oppressive government entity, dramatically and permanently changed the lives of so many Sioux people who knew and remembered the Old Brulie; I was one of them.

Our subsequent move to Iowa was a shock to me. My brother and I were not allowed to go to the Mesquakie tribal school, because we were not members of that nation. The first semester, our mother sent us to Catholic school.

My only comfort in this cold, strange place was that my brother's third grade class was in the same room as my fourth grade. I was taken aback to see so many non-Indian people in one place. Everyone there was white, except for my brother and me. (At Lower Brule, there was only one white family of kids.) Everybody in Iowa seemed to have blue eyes, blond hair and bluish white skin.

This intimidated me so badly that all I could do for the first week of my classroom experience was to keep my head down on my desk and not look at anyone. I hated being in a classroom full of foreign people, strange to me, unfamiliar-looking, talkative and loud. I never knew what to say, or never seemed to know exactly what they were talking about. Moreover, the fourth grade was away from the door, over by the windows; I felt trapped! My only consolation in this foreboding, alien schoolroom dominated by a gray-faced lady with wire rims and a big, long, black robe to the floor, was that my brother, who understood me, was in my eyesight.

The torture and tensions were so intense sometimes that I would look outside the windows and see the sparrows, robins, blue jays and crows flying in the trees. I would wish to be a feather on one of their wings, and would wish they could fly me back to the safety and security of Old Brulie, where I could play on her dusty roads once again; where I could be happy again! If only she weren't buried in that watery grave, so heartlessly created in the name of "progress" by the United States.

Perhaps others don't perceive it, but I believe that my experience of cultural discomfort and grief over my lost village on the banks of the Missouri River exists on the continuum which began with the first voyage of Lewis and Clark in 1804. Their idea of expansion, domination and Manifest Destiny still takes its toll in modern times. As Native people, as Ikce Wicasta, we have been culturally, linguistically, religiously, environmentally and legally brutalized by those who would claim to be our bridge to what they term "civilization."

As a contemporary descendant of the "savages" they so feared and sought to "civilize," I seek a place in my soul where I can heal from historical, multigenerational and personal sorrows begun by the voyage of Meriwether Lewis and William Clark. I believe that we, like the river, cannot really be dominated and conquered, in spite of dramatic changes imposed upon us. Just as the river eventually will take its natural course, despite "civilized" man's attempts to tame it, I wish to find a course of survival as well; I wish to find a way to forgive the day on which the Voyage of Discovery sailed and the history that ensued. I wish to find a place in my spirit where I can pray for those who have challenged me and my people. Mitakuyepi Owas!

The Renaming of a Nation
Lydia Whirlwind Soldier

In 1803, an incredible burst of stars fell out of the eastern indigo sky; hundreds, maybe thousands blazed spectacularly bright, leaving behind glowing trails. Native star-gazers considered this to be a sign. Something in the universe warned of a great disaster approaching, something that would begin in the east at the Mnisose, the river. It would bring sickness, starvation and death. To the Lakota, the Mnisose is Grandfather River. This immense artery is the source of life to the northern lands.

Mnisose, nomadic, serene,
sometimes violent
has seen stars fall
leaving black holes in the sky

It has heard the prairie wolves
now extinct, it has seen the smoke
rise, stretch along earth's rim
trapping the Sicangu in the low hills
it has seen agony and mindless violence
rise and fall against "the people"

This was the time when the United States had purchased the land stretching from the Mississippi to the Rocky Mountains. It was known as the Louisiana Purchase. It had been bought for 3 cents an acre from the French. It did not seem illegal to the Europeans to be selling and buying land that did not belong to them. William Clark and Meriwether Lewis, both military men, had been commissioned to explore the Mnisose. They were to map the land and to gather information on the plants and the animal species and the people of these lands.

Canwape Nanbleca Wi - May 1804

The Corps of Discovery, as this expedition was named, was to leave from St. Louis, Missouri, explore the Mnisose to its source and its tributaries, and find a northwest passage, a water route to the Pacific Ocean. Thomas Jefferson, the president of the United States, envisioned the expansion of population, commerce and trade for the growing nation.

from this narrow twisted place
mythical American history is born
like the rings in a great oak, imbedded deeply

19

year after year, generation after generation
directly, indirectly, it poisons and shapes
America's collective consciousness.

Lewis and Clark met the Kickapoo, Osage, Oto, Ottawa, Ponca, Arkikra, Missouri and Yankton Nations on their way up the river. The peoples of what is now Missouri, Kansas, Nebraska and South Dakota. Lewis and Clark delivered speeches, and expressed the wishes of the government. Peace medals were given and paper chiefs were selected for each tribe. They told the tribes that the land belonged to the United States, to their "Great White Father" who lived in the east. Shotguns and cannon were fired from their great arsenal to show their power. A Yankton newborn was wrapped in the US flag and paternalism for Native tribes was born.

the soil you see is not ordinary soil
it is the dust of the blood,
the flesh and bones of our ancestors...
The land, as it is, is my blood and my dead
it is consecrated...
    Standing Bear, Sicangu Lakota

They left their calling cards, peace medals, the new order of the Plains. They gave papers to the friendly Indians, but Washington would barely ever hear of or recognize these commissions. The people were told that the "Great White Father" wanted "his children" to live in peace, to follow his counsel and that the "Great Spirit" would smile on their nations. There were promises of friendship and promises that their homes would always be in this territory. The Indians believed them.

destiny held in the stars
ancient nations doomed
kegs of rum legitimize theft and slaughter
of nations, ordered to America's wastelands
like the 6,000,000 who could not escape
Hitler's grasp, they would suffer starvation, disease,
grief and death

This was the beginning of the surrogate parents, the "Great White Father" and "Great Spirit." It is a paternalistic way to dismantle Native cultures. This was the beginning of bureaucratic regulations and hierarchical powers of the government that would dictate what was in the "best interest" of tribal people. It was the beginning of a long line of injustices, and the collapse of independence and personal autonomy. Native cultures and the Native languages would become targets of control. The government would force the Natives onto small pieces of land. They would not be free to travel. Their beautiful ceremonies would be forbidden. There would be no freedom to self-govern. Self-naming, self-definition and self-identity would encounter vigorous resistance from those who came to "save" the indigenous people. The Christian churches would rush in to join this political force and they would keep the Natives close and in control.

The Corps of Discovery traveled on, skirting sandbars and piles of driftwood collecting in the river. A member of the expedition wrote in his journal: "This immense river waters the fairest portions of the globe. This garden of Eden stretches across the horizon." They hunted and killed many buffalo, sometimes eating only the tongues and leaving the rest of the carcass for scavengers in this land of plenty. They experienced intense heat, mosquitoes, and thunder and lightning storms.

Mnisose
repository to all
lingering spring flowers
shadows of cottonwoods ribbon
the banks
intimate to all life around
swish of waves and bends in
the Mnisose
flash in the crimson light of sunset
and faint flicker of stars in the dawn

They reached present-day Pierre, South Dakota, where they met the Teton Nation, known as the Lakota. They stayed among the Lakota for seven days. They would later say that the Lakota were newcomers on the plains who had recently migrated to the west. This would be their way to negate the Lakotas' rightful place in this blue-domed prairie cathedral; to legitimize land theft and the occupation of Lakota lands. The Lakota were a powerful nation to be defeated. To them, the Lakota chiefs, Buffalo Medicine, Partisan and Black Buffalo, were only obstacles. They forced Lewis and Clark to pay a toll and they tried to confiscate their canoes. "These were a savage race, we will make them feel the dependence on our will for their survival." Again, their intentions were written in a journal.

did they see themselves as murderers?
those shadows creeping up the Mnisose
they came to take and
change forever
this land of nature-scented beauty
did they believe they were divinely ordained
by the "Great Spirit"?
those foreboding silhouettes

foreign urban beings, sent by the
"Great White Father"
ethnic cleansing begins
fragrant sage in bloom and treasure prism
sunsets fractured, disease of white supremacy
bitter and mean unleashed.

Each tribe was labeled "savage" in the journals of Lewis and Clark. They could not refrain from judgment and from embracing the fallacy of superiority. Already productive cross-cultural communications were trampled upon. There was intolerance from a "nation of immigrants."

Canwape Kasna Wi - September, 1804

They reached the Mandan and Hidatsa villages. The ice closed in on them and they spent the winter near present-day Bismarck, North Dakota. Here they met the Gros Ventres and the "most friendly, most disposed, 'savages,' the Mandan people." "We wish to be at peace, if we eat, you eat, if we starve you shall too starve," the Mandan people were told. Expedition members were given buffalo robes, dried buffalo meat and crops that the indigenous people had cultivated for centuries, corn, squash and beans. They were also given diseases brought to the Mandan by French trappers.

did these American forebears
look into the eyes of the indigenous?
or were they like the northern lights
obscured streaks of light
raw and cold
floating and disappearing into the cold night?

A Shoshoni woman, Bird Woman, also known as Sacajawea, her newborn baby, Jean Baptiste, and her husband, Toussaint Charbonneau, joined the expedition at the Mandan village. Like most Frenchmen who had come to our country, he had learned the Native languages. Sacajawea, with her fortitude, calm and poise, became an indispensable member of the expedition for several reasons. Having a woman with the expedition made it apparent that their intentions were peaceful. She spoke the Shoshoni language, which would help the expedition obtain horses from her people to traverse the mountains. Finally, like most Native women, she was an accomplished homemaker. With her wealth of knowledge and experience, she enriched their diet of fresh meat with roots, berries and seeds, and preserved them for future use by drying. She would spend nearly two years with the expedition and she would be mentioned in the journals of Lewis and Clark at times as Sacajawea, but most often she would be referred to as a "squaw," and sometimes as "the woman," and then, finally, as "Janey" – "a real human being."

Sacajawea
teen mother, and second wife
gentle, mild interpreter
carried her son across the prairies and mountains
led this expedition across a continent
Native woman,
chased the whitemens' dream
maybe not by choice
her name became the most prominent
on this epic journey

Wihakakta Cepapi Wi - April

Miles and distances were told in seasons. They left the Mandan village the following spring. They saw the range of Shining Mountains to the west, and the snow-covered peaks and golden sunsets of the future states of Montana and Idaho. There they met the Shoshoni and Nez Perce nations. They mapped the "new" territory that "Foot of civilized man never trod," according to a journal report. They stayed near the river for fear of Indians and wild beasts. Although every river and landmark had already been named by the original inhabitants, every member's name was affixed to the land. Their names were carved into trees, rivers, streams and mountains as they traveled west.

Maybe it is not so amazing that Lewis and Clark misunderstood the traditions of the Native people. Before the explorers reached the Yellowstone, they came upon burial platforms and they assumed that Natives placed their dead on these platforms because they believed that the "Great Spirit" (a term the newcomers invented) would come and take the deceased to the Spirit land. In reality, tribal people prepared their loved ones for their spirit journey, and placed them on platforms so they could return more quickly to Unci Maka (Grandmother Earth). It is a very simple concept, and there is nothing mysterious in it. Maybe labeling the Natives as superstitious, primitive and savage, made it easier to justify the theft of a nation.

The expeditioners traveled through the mountains and what they considered to be deserts. They were amazed at the beauty of the land. The water of Mnisose had cut bluffs and white sandstone cliffs that were over three hundred feet high – "unclaimed territory," they called it. They caught whitefish and trout, and hunted buffalo, antelope, mule deer, bear and elk.

if this land has a soul
it is in the river, its
deep rushing water danced across the breadth
of this land
it wove magical stories

shifting patterns caressed the
weathered pines, fragrant cedar
the mountains and prairies
it carried star reflections and rainbow ceremonies
if this land has a soul it is in the river, it
did not turn against
those who came
to civilize it

Timpsila Itkahca Wi - June

Here there was a clash between reality and hope. It is here where Sacajawea got very ill and nearly died. There was concern for her baby, but maybe
more concern for the expedition. Who would speak to the Shoshoni people for
horses? Who would guide them over the mountains? She was given hot sulfur
water to drink, which seemed to help her. Holding Jean Baptiste to her breast,
she willed herself to live.

Wasuton Wi - August

They searched over the land for the Shoshoni. "Let us fly to the mountains,
living lean and hungry lives." With a white flag, a sign of peace, they finally
found Sacajawea's people in the Bitterroot Range of the Rocky Mountains. Although finally reunited with her people, Sacajawea decided to travel on with
the expedition. They rested for several days, and traded for horses to continue
on.

Canwape Gi Wi - September

The Mnisose became swifter as they approached the snow-peaked rugged
Rocky Mountains. On the western horizon, they saw the foothills covered with
the evergreen forests of pine and juniper and peaceful fields of mountain flowers. Big Horn sheep clung to the rocky crags, and herds of buffalo roamed
freely. They hunted the whitetail deer, elk, the black bear and the grizzly. They
reached the Bitterroot River. They were tested on their knowledge and survival
skills; on the edge of starvation they were forced to eat dogs and horses. They
found they would rather eat dog than elk meat. On they traveled, on to Clear
Water River. They wandered lost and were found by the Nez Perce people and
fed. These were the first whitemen to be seen by the Nez Pierce.

They were to cross these mountains to reach the shores of the Pacific. But
first, they searched for the Great Falls, the landmark which would show them
that they were on the right trail. They heard the tremendous roar of the Great

Falls, before they saw them. They portaged the Great Falls going a greater distance than they had planned.

Great Falls
enchanting dream
cool rainbow mists
rise and fall on the wind
freshwater springs cascade
into limestone beds
home to great grizzlies
and buffalo
home of the Plateau and
Great Basin people

They encountered grizzly bears, storms, flash floods, hailstones and illness, always illness, and the daunting mountains still stretched before them. They met the Shoshoni, Salish, Nez Perce and Blackfeet people as they travel over the mountains.

The first whiteman who came to our country,
we let them pass, never made war on them,
never broke that promise.
We were friends with the whiteman
        Chief Joseph

Waniyetu Wi - November

They reached the Continental Divide where the river flowed west. They traveled on to the Columbia River. There were salmon beyond belief. They saw Mt. Hood. The air was cooler and the forests of spruce and pine were streaked with early snow. The sun rose further north every morning. Clouds of geese pointed their arrow heads north. They were finally back on the map. They passed through the Columbia Gorge and into the rain forest. For the first time, they saw people in cedar clothing. However, they also saw some who had abandoned their Native clothing for calico and wool. The Natives lived in plank houses. The seacoast was densely-populated. Some of the Natives spouted cuss words learned from the English who had already explored and settled the area. They could smell the salt air, and feel the currents and tides. They barely made it to the west coast before winter moons again closed in on them.

the stars are silent and pale
mist hangs like a silent prayer
it turns itokagatakiya (toward the spirit land)

reaches out,
to bathe the land,
to draw upon its innate source
ink-tipped wings of snow geese
follow when the silver moon calls and
snowflakes like uncharted galaxies
appear in the autumn mist

Wanicokan Wi - December

They spent the winter near the ocean and rocky coast. They voted to camp for the winter on the south side of the Columbia river, next to the Spruce River. The black slave, York, voted 67 years before blacks would be allowed to vote. Sacajawea voted a century before Indian women could vote. They had become a democratic unit for that brief period. They named their winters quarters Fort Clatsop, after a Native tribe in the area.

The winters were less severe than on the northern plains, yet every day was wet, steaming and uncomfortable. They awoke to silent days, a sky covered by slate-gray clouds hanging over the mountains and valleys. In the gray of the day, they walked the well-worn and rain-rutted trails to hunt. They ate nothing but elk meat, which they tired of very quickly. They ran out of all supplies but guns, lead and powder. They hoped that a ship would come to the harbor so members of the expedition could carry home the species they had collected. But no ship was sighted for the five months they were on the coast.

Lewis
retreated within the black sky
and salty cool air of early morning
and late evening
caught in the wake
of great rivers and icy barriers

He could not reach beyond
cavernous obstacles
and deep silence of snow
stole a canoe, struck an Indian
searched for greater meaning
to fill that space flat and empty
when everything and nothing is the same
Outsider breaking his own rules.

Istawicayanzan Wi - March

When a strong steady breeze from the south finally brought spring, they prepared for their return trip. Still, there would be much hunger and illness.

Canwape Nanbleca Wi - May

On their return trip, they again met the Nez Perce. The Nez Perce, who selectively bred their horses for beauty and speed. They gave the expedition horses as gifts. They were considered to be the most hospitable and honest by the expedition. They vowed they would be friends to the Nez Perce forever.

To live in harmony was a dream.
The whitemen did not learn to be good students.
They did not learn in their dealings with the Native peoples.
They did not learn the lessons they were taught.
       Native Chief

Canpasapapi Wi - July

As they left the mountains, they separated into smaller units to explore the country. Clark inscribed his name in a cliff and named a landmark, Pompy's Tower, and a nearby creek, Baptiste's Creek, after Sacajawea's son. He named a river and a mountain peak after Sacajawea. Here they met with the Blackfeet people. The most powerful people in the northern and Canadian plains. These warrior knights had the most horses, and guns, and connections to traders in Canada. According to Lewis, they shared dinner with some Blackfeet warriors and camped together. During the night a confrontation ensued with the Blackfeet over a rifle; two of the Blackfeet were killed. According to Blackfeet oral history, two young Blackfeet boys entered the Lewis and Clark camp. One boy was twelve, the other thirteen. They tried to leave the camp during the night and one was stabbed and the other shot. According to Lewis and Clark, they barely escaped the Blackfeet with their lives. They rejoined the expedition. Fearing for their lives, they traveled 120 miles to escape the Blackfeet.

There is no hiding place
even in the darkest places
even in the ghost places
the stars wait
bundles of war arrows wait
while the owl hunts on silent wings
the hawk shadows approach

August 17, they returned to the Mandan villages where they left Sacajawea and her family. William Clark asked to adopt the baby, but the baby was too young to leave his mother. However, after Sacajawea's death, Clark would take responsibility and become the permanent legal guardian of Sacajawea's two children.

Message to the "Great White Father"
Tell your white children,
those who come onto our lands,
did not keep your word.
    Chief Joseph

Again they passed through Teton territory. Buffalo Medicine stood on the river bank and watched them pass. We do not know Black Buffalo's mind, but we do know that he was unfamiliar with this new European culture, unfamiliar with the skillful exploitation and manipulation of these newcomers, and that this was just the beginning. We also know that very few were chosen to become chief in Lakota society. Chiefs were chosen as leaders by the people because of their outstanding commitment to Lakota values. A chief had to be a reasonable man, who would listen to his people, and weigh all arguments for the truth and survival of the people. A message was given to Buffalo Medicine by the expedition: "Inform your nation we will not forget the treatment." Black Buffalo responded with 3 strokes on the green earth, an oath to an enemy.

That promise was held.

The Corps of Discovery traversed the lands from St. Louis to the Pacific coast and back again, 4,162 miles, and they collected 122 species of animals, 178 plants never described for science. They traveled 2 1/2 years with 40 people and lost only one person to disease. They opened the way for a tide of five generations to flood the country bought for 3 cents an acre.

In the following century, white buffalo hunters would kill all but 550 buffalo, leaving the Natives without their food source. The Natives would be murdered, or left to die of the diseases the foreigners had brought with them, and they would be driven to reservations on the most arid and desolate land in the country. Soon after, the lands of the reservations would diminish until the tribes were living on small islands. The whites would still look hungrily at all that was left and lobby Congress to open reservation lands to land-hungry immigrants.

The earth is the mother of all people
and all people should have equal rights upon it.
You might as well expect the rivers to run backwards

as that any man who was born free should be contented
when penned up and denied liberty
to go where he pleases
Chief Joseph

They completed their journey and returned to St. Louis and were received as heroes. They had traveled the far, the unknown, for destiny. They had thought of the land as fierce and hostile, yet they had found beauty. They had devoted hours of their time, patiently drawing maps of the land which the Natives knew like the backs of their hands. They had found many tribes of people who they did not try to understand. Instead, they had preconceived notions which they would use to justify the taking of the land. The two distinctly different cultures would never learn to understand each other without judgment. They could not understand how the Indian could live simply and deeply, and enjoy each moment of life, and the Indian would never understand why the whiteman carries a constant worry about the future, and the hoarding of earthly goods. They could not understand why the Indians had reverence for life, why the Indians took only what they needed and would not waste a morsel of their hunts in this land of plenty.

The members of the expedition were awarded double pay and given land. Many members of the expedition disappeared into the mists of time. York continued on as a slave. When he was not paid or given land, he asked, "What do I get; how about my freedom?" Clark would not give him his freedom, but instead he beat him and kept him in slavery, not releasing him until five years later.

I am going to venture that man who sat on the ground
in his tipi meditating on life and its meaning,
accepting the kinship to all creatures, and acknowledging unity
with the universe of things, was infusing into his being
the true essence of civilization.
Luther Standing Bear, Oglala Lakota

William Clark became the Superintendent of Indian Affairs. Merriwether Lewis became the governor of Louisiana Territory. Eventually, he descended into depression. He intended to travel to Washington, DC, and had a layover at Chickasaw Bluffs. What must have been on his mind in the stifling silence when he asked that a buffalo robe be laid on his floor before he killed himself? Perhaps that he had a hand in the killing of nations? Who was the heathen nation here? Who was the savage? It is said that Clark never again referred to Lewis's death without tears in his eyes.

In those buffalo days
they saw something new in
the emerald green valleys and tawny hills
all there for the use or destruction of a new nation

animal nations,
species never seen before,
the coyote and prairie wolf, antelope,
prairie dogs, turkey, and elk, black-footed ferret,
bighorn sheep and the great grizzly
buffalo herds by the thousands
grazed on the boundless horizon

in the sky of clear blue and cotton fluffed clouds
the winged nations flourished,
flocks of geese filled the skies
pelicans and whooping cranes fished
along the Mnisose
now gone forever the
passenger pigeon and Carolina parakeet

from the springs flowed sweet water into
rivers and lakes
great numbers of water nations
fish, otter and shrimp
beaver and muskrat in their lodges
somehow persevered from those days

grapes, plums, cherries and currants in every ravine
vegetables and medicines of the plant nations
many species now only spirit memories
as the face of death stepped
onto the shores of the Mnisose

In those buffalo days
Mnisose was the Grandfather River.
It was, is still an artery to the paradise
we call home.

BIBLIOGRAPHY
Bakeless, John. (Ed.). (1964). *The Journals of Lewis and Clark*. New York:
    Signet Classic Press.
Thomasma, Kenneth. (1997). *The Truth about Sacajawea*. Jackson, WY:
    Grandview Publishing Company.

The Missing Voices
Elden Lawrence

The saga of the Lewis and Clark expedition is truly an American story for the American mainstream enthusiast. Yet while it is acclaimed as one of the great historic events in American history, most indigenous people of this land regard it as a continuation of an invasion practice that has historic roots going back to the Crusades. Lewis and Clark may have been discovering "America" for Euro-Americans, but the indigenous people were already here, living in the so-called "wilderness." It is unlikely that many knowing indigenous people receive inspiration from the journey of the Corps of Discovery. Rather, many will regard it, like the voyages of Columbus, as an infamous event.

The discovery of America was the result of Old World developments, namely the Crusades, the Renaissance, and the rise of absolute monarchs that ruled nation states. The First Crusade was a military expedition, launched in 1096 after Pope Urban II summoned Western Christendom to wrest the Palestine Holy Land away from the Moslem Turks. Over the next 200 years, Western Europe embarked on its first ventures in colonialism and conducted seven major crusades in an effort to establish Christian religious civilizations. Although there were some temporary successes, the Crusades failed to bring about complete and permanent Christian rule in other lands, as the last crusader stronghold fell in 1291. The Columbian voyages 200 years later were in many ways a continuation of historic beliefs and practices.

It is important, therefore, to understand the original beliefs and practices which established the pattern of the invasion, and to understand the basic motives which remained much the same down through the centuries.

The Renaissance in Western Europe was a period of great intellectual interest in worldly or non-religious components of civilization. Renaissance scholars placed a great deal of emphasis on reason, questioned authority, and pursued free inquiry. The scholars were particularly interested in the advanced Byzantine and Moslem civilizations initially encountered during the Crusades, as well as being curious about the Greco-Roman culture in the Italian city-states. The Italian city-states had wealthy merchants and rulers and had close contacts with the Byzantine and Moslem worlds, whose riches, resources, and desirable products had also stimulated a desire for exploration and colonization of new areas beyond European shores.

Because of their wealth and security, these merchants and rulers could devote much time, energy, and money to pursuing the arts, sciences, and personal or national aggrandizement. Furthermore, the secular humanist philosophical content that characterized Renaissance thought glorified man as the measure of all things. This outlook encouraged individualism, the pursuit of wealth, fame, and power, and striving for excellence. The famous scientists, artists, capitalist entrepreneurs, adventurers, soldiers of fortune, and conquistadors of the next few centuries were products of this modern European world view.

Near the end of the Middle Ages, the kings were able to extend their authority over the lords and eventually became absolute monarchs. Their royal power was strengthened by the Crusades, as many of the feudal lords were killed, giving rise to a new rank of middle-class merchants. To protect their property and trade, this merchant class supported their kings, resulting in increased nationalistic spirit, with the kings being the symbols of national unity. Nation-states included England, France, Spain, and Portugal. Western Europe secured sufficient wealth to finance voyages of discovery. These voyages were a two-edged sword—the nation-states gained larger colonial empires and the merchants increased their wealth through trade opportunities gained by these expeditions.

Spain financed the Columbus expedition that took him to the Caribbean Islands. Ironically, Columbus never set foot on the American mainland, instead exploring some outlying islands and coasts of Central America and northern South America. Columbus believed that he had reached the West Indies, so he called the indigenous people "Indians." Therefore, we can give Columbus credit for giving us our first stereotypical label. Later, Amerigo Vespucci, another Italian explorer, reached the mainland and declared it a new continent. The new continent, first called "the New World," later became "America." Maybe because Americans didn't want Columbus to be entirely wrong, the name "Indian" has been with us since.

Western Europe was on the threshold of a new era in the 15th century, following the pattern of the early crusades and inspired by the Renaissance spirit. With information obtained from the Columbian voyages, explorers were sent to the New World to search for and secure sources of wealth, obtain more information about the indigenous people, establish trade sources, and, where desired, accomplish colonization. The commercial revolution shifted from the exploration and use of the trade routes of the Mediterranean to the explorations and use of the trade routes of the Atlantic. More specifically, the explorers were commissioned to (1) satisfy their intellectual curiosity and spirit of adventure, (2) establish claims to new lands, (3) secure gold, silver, precious gems, and other valuables, (4) pave the way for settlements and trading, (5) convert the Indians to Christianity, and (6) find a passage through or around the Americas to the Far East.

In 1800, Napoleon Bonaparte secretly obtained the Louisiana Territory from Spain, nullifying the Pinckney Treaty of 1795 between Spain and the United States. That treaty had allowed the United States to use the port of New Orleans as a shipping point for traders. Napoleon suspended that right in 1802, threatening the economy of Western settlers.

President Jefferson quickly dispatched James Monroe and Robert Livingston to negotiate the purchase of New Orleans. Napoleon, instead, offered to sell the entire territory for $15 million. His reasons for selling were (1) he needed the money to carry on the war with Britain, and (2) he could not defend the country while the British controlled the seas, and (3) he had abandoned plans for an American empire.

The U.S. Constitution did not give the president specific power to purchase territory. With the possibility that Napoleon might change his mind, Jefferson used the president's power to make treaties as a way to get around the rules, thus adopting a loose interpretation of the Constitution. Throughout American history, presidents and political leaders have devised ways to usurp laws. Necessity makes laws and necessity breaks laws. As Bismarck said, "Since the life of a state cannot stand still, conflicts become questions of power; whoever has the power in his hands then proceeds according to his will."

On May 14, 1804, Lewis and Clark and the Corps of Discovery party began their expedition to explore the newly-purchased Louisiana Territory. It was a wilderness journey, assuming Indians were part of the "wildness." Daily journals were kept to record all the details of the trip. These eyewitness accounts are reliable reports of what they saw and what they experienced. However, witnessing from a keelboat and walking among the people are two different things. I know white people who have lived next to Indians for two or three generations, and still know very little about them. You cannot begin to understand Indian people until you know something about their culture and heritage. Their language, philosophy, values, beliefs, and the way they process information are at the opposite end of a continuum with the American mainstream. No two cultures are more different.

The Lewis and Clark expedition was just the beginning of a massive invasion that left in its wake disease, death, and starvation, almost totally destroying the way of life of a people who lived with natural law and in harmony with all of creation. Plowed fields, paved streets, buildings, and interstate highways desecrate the bones of our ancestors daily until the land is no longer sacred. Whether one destroys with a stone ax or a massive earth mover, it is still barbaric. I would rather be an "uncivilized savage" than a barbarian. So celebrate the Crusades, the Renaissance, Columbus and all the other explorations, including Lewis and Clark. As for me, I will cast my lot with the elders of my people.

> Every part of this soil is sacred in the estimation of my people.
> Every hillside, every valley, every plain and grove, has been
> hallowed by some sad or happy event in days long vanished.
> The very dust upon which you now stand responds more lovingly to their footsteps than to yours, because it is rich with
> the blood of our ancestors and our bare feet are conscious
> of the sympathetic touch. Even the little children who lived

here and rejoiced here for a brief season will love these somber solitudes and at eventide they greet shadowy returning spirits. And when the last Red Man shall have perished, and the memory of my tribe shall have become a myth among the White Men, these shores will swarm with the invisible dead of my tribe, and when your children's children think themselves alone in the field, the store, the shop, upon the highway, or in the silence of the pathless woods, they will not be alone. At night when the streets of your cities and villages are silent and you think them deserted, they will throng with the returning hosts that once filled and still love this beautiful land. The White Man will never be alone. Let him just and deal kindly with my people, for the dead are not powerless. Dead, did I say? There is no death, only a change of worlds.

Chief Seattle (1854)

Feasting on Lewis and Clark
Craig Howe

It has been 200 years since the Corps of Discovery began its epic journey from Saint Louis to the Pacific Ocean and back. And sometimes I wonder if those of us who have studied the expedition and examined the Lewis and Clark journals still do not know what really happened, especially with regard to our uncritical acceptance of what those journals say—and do not say. In other words, what they present and what they omit. It appears that those journals are often treated with a reverence usually reserved for sacred documents. Rarely are they systematically interrogated or thoroughly questioned.

On the morning of the autumnal equinox of 1804, William Clark looked back toward the Big Bend of the Missouri River and saw a telltale plume of smoke drifting toward the northwest on the early morning breeze. In his journal he wrote: "we observed a great Smoke to the S W. which is an Indian Signal of their having discovered us." He and Lewis had hoped that their expedition could pass undetected through Teton territory. But it didn't. And for the following seven days and nights, the expedition and the Tetons haltingly carried on a running negotiation as the three expedition boats navigated a complex course through Teton territory. Clark, the expedition's chief journalist, subsequently described the Tetons as a terrifying and treacherous people. His words shaped a negative image of Tetons that has persisted for two centuries.

It is not possible to ascertain what actually happened between the 23rd and the 30th of September, 1804, as Lewis and Clark negotiated passage of their expedition through Teton territory. But that week's events have been presented by historians as pivotal in both the expedition's journey and in the history of the United States. Moreover, nearly all post-expedition chroniclers have uncritically used Clark's accounts to create a heroic image of Lewis and Clark and of their expedition, and a malicious image of the Teton people. A close reading of Clark's writings and of other expedition texts, however, reveal factual and logical inconsistencies that suggest alternative explanations of that week's interactions between the expedition and the Tetons. The Tetons, it turns out, employed an array of strategies in attempting to get trade goods from the well-stocked expedition. Some of their strategies were indeed confrontational, but the texts do not support a characterization of them as malicious. The actions of Lewis and Clark, on the other hand, may have been far less heroic than historians have heretofore allowed.

So this essay will do two things. First, it will briefly examine some strategies that the Tetons used in response to the presence of the Lewis and Clark expedition in their lands, and explore how modern-day descendants of those Tetons—including activists and other like myself—are mirroring those strategies in responding 200 years later to the bicentennial celebration of the Lewis and Clark expedition. Then it will rock the bicentennial keelboat of the Corps of Discovery by arguing that, contrary to 200 years of mainstream narratives, Lewis and Clark took Lakota hostages in order to insure safe passage of their expedition through the territory of the peoples Clark called the "troublesome Tetons."

The phrase "Troublesome Tetons" is from Clark's journal entry on August 25th, 1806, as the Corps of Discovery was on its rapid descent down the Missouri River to St. Louis. That evening, as the Corps of Discovery camped about 10 miles upriver from today's Oahe Dam spillway in South Dakota, Clark wrote:

> "At 3 PM we passed the place where we saw the last encampment of Troublesome Tetons below the old ponia village on the SW side" (Moulton, 322).

The encampment Clark was referring to was the Oglala village that the expedition encountered on September 30th, 1804 on their way up the Missouri River. That had been nearly two years earlier. But those 23 months had not diminished Clark's feelings toward the Tetons. He hated them. In a letter to President Jefferson in the spring of 1805, Clark called the Tetons "the vilest miscreants of the savage race" and urged the president to use whatever means were necessary in order to break the Tetons' power and make them dependent on the United States.

The English word "Teton" is a translation of Titonwan, the Lakota name for one of the seven nations of the Oceti Sakowin, or Seven Council Fires. The Tetons are subdivided into seven Lakota tribes: Oglala, Sicangu, Mnikonju, Hunkpapa, Sihasapa, Oohenumpa, and Ita Zipco. For most purposes, the terms "Tetons" and "Lakotas" are interchangeable. In this essay, "Tetons" will refer to the peoples that Lewis and Clark met, and "Lakotas" will refer to their modern-day descendants. Based on the available evidence, it was mostly the territory of the Sicangu tribe that Lewis and Clark passed through on their journey up the Missouri River between the 23rd and 30th of September, 1804, and also on their return downstream in the final days of August, 1806. Today there are still some Sicangu-controlled lands along the Missouri River—most notably within the Lower Brule Indian Reservation—but the majority of their lands are farther west and now constitute the Rosebud Sioux Indian Reservation.

There are five strategies that the Tetons employed in response to the Lewis and Clark expedition in 1804. Those five strategies are theft, demand, exchange, threat, and friendship. Firsthand accounts of these strategies may be gleaned from the pages of the expedition journals. On September 24th, 1804, for instance, John Ordway recorded an instance of theft:

About 7 o'clock we saw Colter who had been with the horse on an Island south side. He called for the pirogue to take in the game he had killed which was 2 elk and a deer. While they were dressing and getting the meat on board, the Indians stole the horse and some salt out of his bag etc.

The next day, after a formal council during which Lewis and Clark gave gifts to three Teton chiefs, Ordway recorded an instance of a Teton demand strategy, writing that "the chiefs did not appear to talk much until they had got the goods, and then they wanted more, and said we must stop with them or leave one of the pirogues with them as that was what they expected."

That same day, Clark recorded an example of an exchange strategy:

About 11 o'clock the 1st and 2nd chief came. We gave them some of our provisions to eat, they gave us Great quantities of meat.

Clark also recorded an instance of a Teton threat strategy that occurred later that afternoon:

As soon as I landed 3 of their young men Seased the cable of the Perogue, one Soldr Huged the mast, and the 2d Chief was exceedingly insolent both in words & jestures to me declareing I should not go off, Saying he had not received presents Suffient from us —I attempted to passify but it had a contrary effect for his insults became So personal and his intentions evident to do me injurey, I Drew my Sword.

On the positive side of the ledger, all of the expedition journalists wrote at length about the wonderful hospitality that the Tetons extended to them, mentioning in particular the large feasts on the evenings of September 26th and 28th. An excerpt from Clark's account of September 26th, 1804, illustrates this friendship strategy of Tetons:

About 5 o'clock I was approached by 10 well Dressed young men with a neet Buffalow Roab which they Set down before me & requested me to get in they Carried me to their Council Tents forming 3/4 Circle & Set me down betwn 2 Chef ... a large fire was made on which a Dog was cooked, & in the center about 400 wt of Buffalow meat which they gave us ... an old man rose & Spoke approveing what we had done. Requesting us to take pity on them &C

So these are five strategies that the Tetons employed in 1804 to respond to the Lewis and Clark expedition. Now, nearly 200 years later, Lakota descendants of those Tetons are employing those same strategies in response to the bicentennial observances of the expedition.

The modern-day equivalent of the theft strategy is when Lakotas assert that the bicentennial is not about Lewis and Clark, or about Lakotas in the early 1800s. Instead, they say it is about the legacy of genocide and colonialism, racism, oppression and loss of land that Lakotas have endured and are still dealing with today. Lakotas want to use the bicentennial as an opportunity to address these current and ongoing issues instead of celebrating, honoring or applauding a small group of non-Lakota men who lived 200 years ago.

If monies are spent on bicentennial activities that are related to Tetons, then Lakotas enacting the demand strategy want a percentage of that money for their tribes. They demand that public works projects, such as road improvements and construction of interpretive buildings, have some financial benefit to the tribes on whose lands the tourists will travel.

The exchange strategy of Lakotas is manifested in wish to participate in bicentennial activities, especially those that bear on interpreting Lakota history and culture. In so doing, Lakotas will not only inform and educate tourists about Lakotas in the past and present, but they will also protect sacred sites and knowledge.

Some Lakotas on the other hand, wish to disrupt the bicentennial activities, to rock the keelboat, so to speak. These Lakotas threaten to stage protests and to engage in acts of civil disobedience. In so doing, they are reenacting the threat strategy of the Teton relatives 200 years ago.

And at the other end of the spectrum, some Lakotas are employing the friendship strategy through affiliation with the Tribal Circle of Elders, a group of Indian individuals who are working closely with the National Park Service and other federal and state organizations to promote awareness of the bicentennial, particularly in the areas of tourism and education. It is a collaborative effort that seeks to promote a series of well-organized events commemorating the bicentennial, and to avoid confrontational situations.

So there is this nice symmetry: Tetons responding to the expedition in 1804, and Lakotas using the same strategies to respond to the expedition's celebration 200 years later. One of the Teton strategies was to *feast* the Corps of Discovery; today, Lakotas *feast on* the Corps of Discovery by responding to its bicentennial.

But us 21st Century Lakotas have one other strategy for responding to both the expedition and its bicentennial—a strategy that was not an option for our ancestors. That strategy is to reinterpret the events of 1804, to interrogate the original texts and subsequent "histories" that now constitute the mainstream narrative. This is a daunting task, fraught with academic and professional dangers, but that should not deter us from undertaking it.

So let's rock the Lewis and Clark keelboat by feasting on this opportunity to reinterpret what happened during the time the expedition was in Teton territory, beginning with a reexamination of the events of September 25th, 1804.

The events of that afternoon continue to be interpreted in a manner that valorizes Clark, and that identifies those events as pivotal in "the whole history of North America."[1] What actually transpired that afternoon we may never know. The evidence available to us consists of two accounts by Clark and one each by John Ordway, Patrick Gass and Joseph Whitehouse. They represent three substantially different versions of that afternoon's events that historians apparently have not grappled with to ascertain what really went on. Instead, historians have selectively pieced them together into a master narrative that mythologizes Clark and the expedition, and demonizes Tetons.

The accounts of that day by Gass and Whitehouse are nearly identical and agree wholly with Ordway's on the sequence and the facts of that afternoon's events. On the other hand are Clark's two accounts, both of which present substantially different sequences and facts. Clark's two accounts also differ from each other in many ways. So in the absence of other evidence, the Gass, Whitehouse, and Ordway version of sequences and facts appears to be most correct. If that is the case, then Clark's accounts are both incomplete and misleading. Historians and students of the Lewis and Clark expedition, however, continue to rely primarily on Clark's accounts and to ignore the discrepancies between them, and between them and the other three journalists' accounts.

A close and critical reading of the five accounts suggest that the sequences and circumstances of the events of September 25th, 1804 were as follows. Somewhere between 30 and 50 Tetons gathered on a sand bar in the mouth of the Bad River at present-day Fort Pierre, South Dakota. The expedition had erected a flag pole and an awning under which sat chiefs Black Buffalo, Partisan and Buffalo Medicine, and other high-ranking Tetons. Lewis, Clark, and Cruzatte, a mixed-blood Omaha and Frenchman who served as interpreter, joined the chiefs under the awning and smoked a pipe. Cruzatte translated as Lewis and Clark gave speeches and presented gifts to the Teton dignitaries. The chiefs expressed their dissatisfaction with the quantity of gifts and indicated that the expedition should not proceed upriver until it distributed substantially more goods. Sensing a potentially crippling situation, Lewis tried to impress the Tetons by parading the men and demonstrating his air gun, a brand new rifle that had not been seen before in that country. When those tactics were unsuccessful, he and Clark invited the three chiefs and the top-ranking akicita,[2] or warrior, aboard the keelboat, ostensibly to show them more marvels of science, but actually to ply them with whiskey.

The use of liquor was a common ploy of traders at that time to gain advantage over Indians. Liquor was, according to historian Hiram Crittenden, a "weapon, which, more than any other, was certain of victory in any contest for the favor of the Indian."[3] He went on to explain: "It was the policy of the shrewd trader first to get his victim so intoxicated that he could no longer drive a good bargain. The Indian, becoming more and more greedy for liquor, would yield up all he possessed for an additional cup or two."[4] So when their speeches, gifts, parade and gun demonstration were unsuccessful in insuring their safe passage that afternoon, Lewis and Clark decided to get the chiefs and the akicita soldier drunk so as to obtain permission to proceed upriver. They poured each of the visitors "1/2 a wine glass of whiskey," "1/4 a glass of whiskey," or "a draghm" of whiskey.[5]

All three amounts appear in the accounts. Regardless of the specific amount, the captains emptied a whole bottle of whiskey in their effort to implement this strategy, which in the end, failed. Having drunk more than the others, however, Partisan did get intoxicated and began acting erratically. The rest of the Tetons, on the other hand, offered the expedition a large quantity of prime buffalo meat. The captains received the gift but refused to accept a small portion that appeared to be spoiled, a behavior that shamed and infuriated the Tetons. Recognizing their cultural blunder, the captains tried to appease the Tetons by offering them some pork in return, but the situation continued to deteriorate, so the captains ushered their guests off the keelboat and into a canoe. It was not an easy task, as the Tetons were feeling the effects of the whiskey and stinging from insults.

When the canoe landed, Clark stepped onto shore and the three chiefs followed. However, in what apparently was a predetermined delay tactic, Black Buffalo immediately grabbed the bowline and sat down on the bank while the akicita leader wrapped his arms around the mast and refused to leave the canoe. In angry desperation, Clark ordered the keelboat cannons loaded and the crew to prepare to fight. Almost immediately the expedition's considerable firepower was ready. Clark then forcefully told Black Buffalo that his crew were soldiers and would not stand to be detained any longer. Black Buffalo responded that his men too were soldiers and that they would wipe out the expedition to a man, if not that day then over days to come. This infuriated Clark, who launched into a tirade against the Tetons, belittling them and threatening an overwhelming death to them *and* their families.

Recognizing the obstinateness of Clark, yet nevertheless awed by his unimaginable threat of wholesale annihilation of Teton men, women and children, Black Buffalo abandoned his confrontational delay tactic and instead countered with a nonviolent approach, saying that the women and children of his village wished to see the keelboat before the expedition departed. Clark considered this new request and reluctantly consented, but only under the condition that the boats would proceed at least a short distance before nightfall to show that they could not be stopped by the Tetons.

Hesitating only a moment, Black Buffalo let go of the bowline and then said that he understood that the expedition was not a commercial enterprise. He again expressed sorrow that the women and children would not get to see the keelboat and added that they would like to properly welcome the expedition to Teton territory the following day. Wrongly sensing a militaristic delay tactic that would leave his boats vulnerable to attack, but also wishing to reverse the horrendous direction the afternoon's interactions had taken, Clark grudgingly agreed to consider a meeting the next day, but demanded that four Tetons, including Black Buffalo and Buffalo Medicine, return to the keelboat as insurance against possible sabotage.

The Tetons willingly consented, so Clark and his canoe crew returned to the keelboat with the two chiefs—Black Buffalo and Buffalo Medicine—and two other Teton men as virtual hostages. The three-boat flotilla then retreated from its exposed position at the mouth of the Bad River and proceeded north a short distance to where a well-situated island offered a relatively safe location to anchor for the night.

The idea of "holding" a few influential chiefs or even young people as security for the expedition had been spelled out in Jefferson's June 20, 1803, letter of instructions to Lewis. In that letter, Jefferson not only encouraged the established practice of sending important chiefs to Washington to witness the military might and overwhelming population of the United States, but he also suggested that young people be sent back East in order to be properly educated. Such actions would not only benefit the Indians, he wrote, but also "give some security to your own party."[6]

Considering that the expedition was vastly outnumbered that Tuesday afternoon and that the Tetons appeared ill-disposed toward its continuation upriver, Clark's decision to retain a few influential leaders aboard the keelboat as some measure of insurance against possible attack seems logical. Nevertheless, taking hostages was an affront to Jefferson's instruction to treat the Siouxs in a friendly manner and certainly was not the sort of thing that heroic or honorable men did. That is why it is feasible that the expedition journalists did not explicitly mention that hostages were taken. It is only through careful and critical analysis that we can read between the lines of the journalists' texts to decipher the story of what might have happened but was and has been held captive on those pages for nearly two hundred years.

Five days later, on Sunday the 30th of September, 1804, two events occurred that are directly related to, and resolve, this hostage argument. The first was that the expedition encountered a Teton village—most likely an Oglala camp—that proved to be the last and farthest north of the Teton villages along the Missouri River.[7] Beyond that Oglala village the expedition would leave Teton territory and enter the land of the Arikaras. The Oglala villagers wished to meet, greet and feast the expedition, but the captains refused their invitation. They did, however, speak briefly to them from the keelboat before proceeding on toward Arikara territory with Buffalo Medicine still aboard.

Not long before nightfall the second event occurred. The wind apparently picked up, creating high waves that reportedly frightened Buffalo Medicine so much that he asked to be put ashore. Before he started his walk back to his nation, the captains gave Buffalo Medicine some gifts and, according to one of Clark's reports, smoked a pipe with him. The expedition then continued its rapid ascent toward the Arikaras. At first glance, there is nothing remarkable about this event. But upon reflection, it appears extremely fortuitous—from the viewpoint of the expedition—that the wind blew so strong that it scared Buffalo Medicine off the keelboat. When viewed in relation to this hostage hypothesis, however, the high waves are necessary to resolve the situation. If Buffalo Medicine was being held hostage in order to insure the expedition's safe passage through Teton territory, then once the last Teton village was passed his presence was no longer useful. But they could not simply throw him overboard—if for no other reason than the fact that their return journey to St. Louis necessarily passed through Teton territory and there undoubtedly would be repercussions. Therefore, the captains had probably promised Buffalo Medicine that he would be released before the expedition entered Arikara territory and perhaps had also agreed to compensate him for being detained as Clark's report suggests:

> He [Buffalo Medicine] got his gun and informed us he wished to return, that all things were clear for us to go on, we would not see *any* more Tetons etc. We repeated to him what had been said before and advised him to keep his men away. Gave him a blanket, a knife and some tobacco, smoked a pipe and he set out.[8]

The high wind and frightening waves, then, were the excuses that the expedition journalists used to explain why Buffalo Medicine was suddenly put off the keelboat instead of accompanying it upriver, as they earlier had reported was his intention.

Admittedly, this is a conjectural interpretation. But so too are the accounts that chroniclers have been producing for the past two hundred years. Perhaps this metaphorical rocking of the keelboat will shake our faith in the mainstream narrative of the interactions between the expedition and the Tetons, and nourish a reconsideration of the meanings of the expedition's bicentennial.

NOTES
This essay is based on another by Howe that was published under the title "Lewis and Clark among the Tetons: Smoking Out What Really Happened," in *Wicazo Sa Review*, Vol. 19, No. 1 (Spring 2004): 47-72.

[1] "It was a dramatic moment. Had Lewis cried "Fire!" and touched his lighted taper to the fuse of the swivel gun, the whole history of North America might have changed"(Stephen Ambrose, *Undaunted Courage: Meriwether Lewis, Thomas Jefferson, and the Opening of the American West* (New York: Simon & Schuster, 1996), 170).

[2] Akicita is defined by Eugene Buechel, *Dictionary of Teton Sioux* (Pine Ridge, SD: Red Cloud Indian School, 1983), 71, as "A head warrior, one next to a chief, a warrior soldier, a policeman."

[3] Hiram Crittenden, *History of the American Fur Trade of the Far West: A History of the Pioneer Trading Posts and Early Fur Companies of the Missouri Valley and the Rocky Mountains and of the Overland Commerce with Santa Fe* (Stanford, CA: Academic Reprints 1902), 13.

[4] Ibid., 24.

[5] Clark's accounts specify the first two amounts, whereas Ordway specifies the latter amount.

[6] "If a few of their influential chiefs, within practicable distance, wish to visit us, arrange such a visit with them, and furnish them with authority to call on our officers, on their entering the U. S. to have them conveyed to this place at public expense. If any of them should wish to have their young people brought up with us, & taught such arts as may be useful to them, we will receive, instruct & take care of them. Such a mission, whether of influential chiefs, or of young people, would give some security to your own party." (Reuben Thwaites, *Original Journals of the Lewis and Clark Expedition* (New York: Dodd Mead & Company, 1904), 250)

[7] This is the village that Clark referred to in the "Troublesome Tetons" passage quoted earlier.

[8] "we proceeded on under a very Stiff Breeze from the S. E, the Stern of the boat got fast on a log and the boat turned & was very near filling before we got there righted, the waves being very high, The Chief on board was So frightened at the motion of the boat which in its rocking caused Several loose articles to fall on the Deck from the lockers, he ran off and hid himself, we landed he got his gun and informed us he wished to return, that all things were Cleare for us to go on we would not See an more Tetons &c. We repeated to him what had been Said before and advised him to keep his men away, gave him a blanket a Knife & Some Tobacco, Smoked a pipe & he Set out. We also Set Sale and Came to at a Sand bar, & Camped, a very Cold evening. (Garry Moulton (Ed.), *The Definitive Journals of Lewis & Clark: Up the Missouri to Fort Mandan* (Lincoln: University of Nebraska Press, 1987), 130)

Stephen Ambrose's *Undaunted Courage*: A White Nationalist Account of the Lewis & Clark Expedition

Kim TallBear

In true modernist tradition, Stephen E. Ambrose's *Undaunted Courage: Meriwether Lewis, Thomas Jefferson and the Opening of the American West* (Simon & Schuster, 1996), is hailed by some reviewers as a "great book" about "great men." It has been called "the definitive account" of the Lewis and Clark exploration of the American West. In 2004, I saw it prominently displayed in a score of popular bookstores across the country. During this time of surging US nationalism, it is no wonder that *Undaunted Courage* is popular among general readers. While it is perhaps not highly respected among scholars, I think it deserves to be looked at for how it appeals to many people who continue to desire uncomplicated narratives of American history. Such narratives lionize those great men who "discovered" untouched lands and made a Euro-American nation that proudly cultivates "freedom" (a vacuous idea at best when it remains unanalyzed). Therefore, my chief concern in this review is to look at how *Undaunted Courage* appeals to such national politics. I am not concerned with the politics of Lewis and Clark in history, except as they are interpreted and embraced by Americans today.

First, a brief overview of *Undaunted Courage* is in order. Meriwether Lewis and William Clark and their "Corps of Discovery" were conceptualized by President Thomas Jefferson. Setting off in 1804, they were charged with exploring land west of the Mississippi River. They imagined this land as uncharted—undiscovered in a sense—even though many other people (mostly Native and some non-Native) had traversed and inhabited it. In his account of the Corps of Discovery, Ambrose centers Meriwether Lewis, that less nobly-remembered half of the famous duo. Lewis is known to have suffered depression, characterized at one point by Ambrose as manic-depression. He eventually killed himself. For the most part, however, Ambrose presents Lewis as a vision of idealized American masculinity—adventurous, physically powerful, persevering and well-bred.

Undaunted Courage begins with an account of Lewis' birth into a prominent Virginia family in the famed Albemarle County, also home to Jefferson. Lewis was born to a "patriotic" father and a "remarkable" and "tender" mother who could wield a rifle and concocted medicines which she kindly dispensed even to her slaves.[1] Ambrose chronicles Lewis' youthful antics and adventures with just enough concession to historical accounts of expected masculine debauchery.

After the introduction, Ambrose spends two-thirds of the book describing the daily challenges, monotonies, and surprises of the journey. Despite the overly romantic depictions, which I'll discuss shortly, this section of the book is most interesting. It provides sometimes repulsive details about the tastes, smells, textures and diseases encountered by Lewis and Clark and their men. It also provides fascinating detail of the cultural, political and technological aspects of life during that time. As one might expect, however, descriptions of daily life and cross-cultural challenges focus on the experiences of Euro-Americans. Indians' life-ways are described insofar as they clarify how they fit into or complicate the daily lives of whites. Next to nothing is said about the lives and perspectives of slaves, even though Clark's slave, York, accompanied Clark and seems to have participated fully in Corps activities.

The final chapters of the book detail Lewis' life after his return to the "civilized world." He lived a somewhat nomadic life and curiously never succeeded in preparing his journals for publication, despite his great ambition to do so and despite much prodding from Jefferson and the public. He also did very little in the way of substantive work in his role as Governor of Louisiana before he eventually committed suicide.[2]

Ambrose's narrative is full of historical details that make this book an interesting read. The observant reader will see a more complicated story than that of heroes and their individualist pursuits of freedom and discovery. Unfortunately, much of Ambrose's rhetoric insists that he tells a story about great men and great discoveries (despite his more interesting evidence). Following is a passage that typifies his tone:

> The captains would be gone two years, perhaps more. In all that time, in whatever lay ahead of them, whatever decisions had to be made, they would receive no guidance from their superiors. This was an independent command . . . *Lewis and Clark were as free as Columbus, Magellan, or Cook to make their mark on the sole basis of their own judgments and abilities* [emphasis mine].[3]

This is an ironic comparison. Columbus and Cook are chiefly important to many people not for their exploratory genius but for their tragic legacy among indigenous peoples in both hemispheres. Second, even for a biographer, Ambrose's focus on the individual greatness of Lewis and Clark is simplistic. While Lewis and Clark may very well have been able-bodied, intelligent, and adventurous souls, their "own judgments and abilities" did not solely account for how they made "their mark." They were accompanied in the Corps of Discovery by other individuals whose stories and contributions are by and large not told. Ironically, one of the reasons that we don't have the stories of less well-known Corps members is that Lewis suppressed their publication because he feared that they would diminish the market for his own published journals. Lewis and Clark were assisted by individuals—Indian and non-Indian—in crucial and life-saving ways.

On a more abstract level, Lewis and Clark cannot be credited with having had complete intellectual freedom in their decisions. Their beliefs, choices and actions were conditioned by the influential ideas of their day. The frontier-taming discourse that was fundamental in their Euro-American culture compelled them to think inside that story to "make their mark." While Ambrose cannot be expected to give equal time to telling every story, the alternative should not be to claim god-like autonomy for his historical subjects. In this day and age, that seems naïve or simply propagandist.

Just as Ambrose tries to establish Lewis' story as a great man story, he clings to the discovery motif in his romantic history-telling. This is strange because Ambrose admits several times in his narrative that "discovery" does not legitimately characterize the journey. Ambrose frequently admits that Lewis followed well-worn paths and yet he also asserts that Lewis discovered things which he then felt obliged to name.[4] Ambrose relies on the idea of discovery to move his narrative along, even if it means only that Lewis or his men "discovered" natural features or species for their own cultural cohort:

> [Lewis'] notes would have expressed his first reactions to the biomass west of the Mississippi. This was hardly unknown territory; by 1804, the lower reaches of the Missouri had been much traveled. The creeks, islands, and prominent landforms all had names, mainly French. An accurate map existed through the mouth of the Kansas up to the entry of the Platte, and a pretty good map of the country from the Platte to the Mandan villages. But for Lewis it was all new, and he was seeing it with different eyes.
>
> Up to the mouth of the Kansas, most of the flora and fauna were known to science. But there was more than enough of the new to keep Lewis happily busy . . . After the hours at his instruments . . . the hours he got to spend tramping around the prairie on the high ground up from the valley, doing what botanists like to do best—discovering new species—were surely welcome.[5]

With this definition of discovery, I might do as many other Native critics have imagined. I might go to the French countryside, erect a tribal flag and claim "discovery" of those lands and their species. After all, I have never seen the French countryside nor have most of my Dakota cohort, and we have yet to name its natural features.

Yet another tactic of asserting discovery is Ambrose's amusing practice of listing numerous—to my mind—not very consequential firsts of the Lewis and Clark journey. There was the "first" Fourth of July celebration west of the Mississippi, the first US soldier to die west of the Mississippi, the first American to describe the classic Plains tipi, the first American description of the ceremonial dress of the Plains Indian, the first Americans to kill a grizzly, and many more. An especially strange passage is when Ambrose describes a vote among the party as to which site they wanted to camp in for the winter. Ambrose notes that Clark's slave York voted and so did Sacajawea. He inflates the significance of this informal vote among a small group of people:

> This was the first vote ever held in the Pacific Northwest. It was the first time in American history that a black slave had voted, the first time a woman had voted.

But, they weren't in a realm governed by American laws and this was no official American election. Aside from asking how Ambrose knows these were genuine firsts, are they really important historically? This preoccupation with obscure firsts indicates a boyish fantasizing about Lewis and Clark's expedition. More importantly this tactic is another way of laying claim to the West as something discovered, documented, won, and deserved by white men.

The observations which I have heretofore discussed underlie one broad criticism that I have of *Undaunted Courage*. Ambrose's history of the Lewis and Clark expedition, like the expedition itself, is a modernist intellectual project that purports to seek and convey "the" truth. But his interpretation is not necessarily a relevant truth for many Americans, especially many Natives. "Modernity," which began with the Enlightenment, purported to describe and know the world rationally and objectively through observation and description. Such methods were supposed to result in objective and definitive interpretations of the world. Modernity assumes that there is a fundamental truth to be uncovered. And modernist scholarship has been criticized for its moralizing belief in "grand narratives" of historical progress where individual men are the triumphant heroes of our stories.

In keeping with modernist tradition, a primary task of the Corps of Discovery was to observe and describe strange lands in order to provide the Euro-American government and people with knowledge or "truth" about that land. No doubt, Natives and some others already felt they had relevant knowledge about that land. Therefore, Lewis and Clark gave them little in the way of knowledge about their landscape. Ambrose's history also implies definitiveness in most of Lewis and Clark's observations. While Ambrose very occasionally questions the validity of some of Lewis and Clark's perspectives, there is a fundamental perspective that Ambrose seems to share with Lewis and Clark. Lewis and Clark seemed to operate on the principle that the land was essentially empty and unmarked. As other scholars have argued, Indians were not generally realized by white society as fully human at that time; rather, they were considered to be part of the wilderness.[6] From that point of view, it follows naturally that the land was considered empty. Unfortunately, Ambrose's frequent employment of the discovery motif also seems to rest on an assumption (perhaps not all that conscious) that Indians were of the wilderness.

Post-modernism tells us that reading and interpreting historical documents is not a straightforward task. Any Native critic who has been raised on an unhealthy diet of white nationalist American history will agree. Various factors mediate the reader's interpretation. Not only does one's professional training matter, but one's culture, politics, gender, and other orientations filter how one reads and interprets existing ideas and how one produces knowledge. This leads me to mention Ambrose's interpretation of his sources. He does not do much in the way of reckoning with the inherent biases of those sources. Rather, he seems fully invested in their particular cultural lenses and assumptions. This is evident in the following passage:

> The [Lewis and Clark] journals are one of American's literary treasures. Throughout, they tell their story in fascinating detail. They have a driving narrative that is compelling, yet they pause for little asides and anecdotes that make them a delight to read. Their images are so sharp they all but force the reader to put down the book, close the eyes, and see what the captains saw, hear what they heard. . . Theodore Roosevelt, no stranger to adventure, said this about the journals: "Few explorers who saw and did so much that was absolutely new have written of their deeds with such quiet absence of boastfulness, and have drawn their descriptions with such complete freedom from exaggeration."[7]

As the narrative progresses, however, Ambrose uses some of the observations contained in Lewis' journals to concede Lewis' shortcomings. He could be self-centered, sometimes unsympathetic to the concerns of others, and not readily admitting of his own mistakes, all common human shortcomings. In the following passage, Ambrose almost chastises Lewis for his characterization of Sacajawea as apparently lacking sorrow upon returning to her native country. She was of Shoshone people, had been kidnapped five years earlier by Hidatsas, and then traded to Charbonneau whom she had married:

> One wonders too how the man who could be so observant about so many things, including the feelings and point of view of his men, could be so unobservant about Sacagawea's situation. A slave, one of only two in the party, she was also the only Indian, the only mother, the only woman, the only teen-aged person. Small wonder she kept such a tight grip on her emotions.[8]

Such passages indicate that Ambrose knows there are issues of cultural politics to be dealt with in any interpretation of historical texts. However, rather than doing an analysis, he simply "wonders" about Lewis' confusing (to us) attitude toward Sacajawea. Thus Ambrose's reference is particularly unsatisfying because it raises a central issue and then provides no insight.

Ambrose's brief commentary reflects that he has not thought much about such politics. For example, why is Ambrose surprised that Lewis was "so observant" of his men and not of Sacajawea? It seems clear that to Lewis, she was "savage," not fully human or at least not human in the same way he and his men were. The continuous use in the Lewis and Clark journals of terms like "savage" and "squaw" indicate that Indians were daily and casually dehumanized in the language of whites. This would have been the rule of the day—of those who considered themselves to be members of "the civilized world." Therefore, I do not mean to attribute unusual cruelty or ignorance to Lewis or Clark or to imply that they never recorded positive attributes of Indians. They were simply men of their time. Finally, while Ambrose may be moved by Sacajawea's role as a mother or a teenager, those categories were not constructed in the same way in 1804 as they are today and they are not similarly constructed in all cultural contexts. In short, "mother" and "teenager" do not carry the same moral weight in all times and places. Ambrose reads Sacajawea as she might be read in contemporary Western culture, which is not an insightful historical reading. It leaves me wondering if Ambrose highlights at certain points Lewis' shortcomings and racial tensions in the Lewis and Clark expedition mainly to ward off racial analysis of his own narrative.

In his final chapter, Ambrose notes that definitive interpretations of history do not exist because newly discovered historical documentation is always possible. However, new sources are not the most important challenge to what have been held as definitive historical accounts. Native and other anti-colonial and post-modern scholarship has emerged to challenge dominant histories. Such scholarship is widespread and even scholars who might disagree with challenges to dominant histories should convey an understanding that they must not assume but defend their historical focus. Ambrose sometimes notes that Natives made different observations than did Lewis and Clark. However, he implies definitiveness of the Lewis and Clark story and their perspectives by telling that story in a way that assumes that the grand old narrative is still intact. Ambrose only has to improve upon it by bringing Lewis the complicated soul to the fore. For Ambrose, the real story is still a hero's story told by, for, and about white Americans.

I have mentioned that Ambrose displays an adolescent-type awe of Lewis and the expedition. This aspect of his writing is important for understanding how Ambrose is doing nationalist work in *Undaunted Courage*:

> He was a good man in crisis. If I was ever in a desperate situation—caught in a grass fire on the prairie, or sinking in a small boat in a big ocean, or the like—then I would want Meriwether Lewis for my leader. . . . I would instinctively trust Lewis to know what to do . . . Certainly he would be anyone's first choice for a companion on an extended camping trip. Imagine sitting around the campfire while he talked about what he had seen that day.[9]

While such romantic and narrow views of Lewis are somewhat mitigated by Ambrose's other references to Lewis as a complicated character, I am convinced that Ambrose's task here—more than scholarship—is indulging a personal fantasy. The overly romantic Lewis references are so numerous as to undermine Ambrose's other efforts to balance his character in this biography-cum-history. Ambrose dreams of being in the company of one of US history's great men and asks his reader to imagine likewise. Who does he think he speaks to? If I imagine being on an extended camping trip with Lewis, the last thing I would want is to hear him tell tales of his day. Given the descriptions of Lewis' personal demeanor and the living conditions of the day, I mostly imagine how lice-infested, diseased, intolerant, egoistic and moody Lewis must have been. I wouldn't sit within twenty feet of him.

Ambrose increases the romance of the story by using the same omnipotent narration that is employed in fiction. The author describes the characters' thoughts, body language, facial expressions and dispositions in arresting detail because the author imagines them. Consider the following largely imagined account:

> And who can doubt that, as they [Lewis and Clark] stuck out their hands to each other, both men had smiles on their faces that were as broad as the Ohio River, as big as their ambitions and dreams.
>
> Oh! To have been able to hear the talk on the porch that afternoon, and on into the evening, and through the night. There would have been whisky . . . there would have been tables groaning under the weight of port, beef, venison, duck, goose, fish, fresh bread, apples, fresh milk and more.
>
> There were the two would-be heroes with the authentic older hero [Clark's older brother General George Rogers Clark], all three Virginians, all three soldiers, all three Republicans, all three great talkers, full of ideas and images and memories and practical matters, and grand philosophy, of Indians and bears and mountains never before seen. Excitement and joy ran through their questions and answers, words coming out in a tumble.[10]

Unfortunately, we don't have a single word of description of the meeting of Lewis and Clark. While much of the rich detail in *Undaunted Courage* comes from historical documentation, Ambrose admits there is no historical documentation to support this idealized description. Therefore, he relies on imagination to write the passage. Following are two other passages that do not have sufficient historical documentation. Consequently they deteriorate into romantic—bordering on fictional—accounts:

The next day, the expedition passed Boone's settlement. The village consisted of a colony of Kentuckians led by Daniel Boone . . . Did Lewis and Clark meet Daniel Boone? Did they shake his hand? Did he wish them luck, offer advice, or a drink? Did he pass the torch? . . . But had he met Boone, surely Clark would have written about it. And there is no known entry for the day.[11]

At sunset, the men again fired the cannon. It was the first-ever fourth of July celebration west of the Mississippi River.

Perhaps the captains grew philosophical under the influence of the whiskey, as happens to earnest young men carrying heavy responsibilities who find themselves in the Garden of Eden as full dark comes on and the campfire burns down on their nation's birthday. Clark's last journal entry that day: "So magnificent a Senerey . . . in a Country thus Situated far removed from the Civilised world to be enjoyed by nothing but the Buffalo Elk Deer & Bear in which it abounds & Savage Indians." Possibly the captains puzzled over why God had created such a place and failed to put Virginians in it, or put it in Virginia.[12]

Perhaps the captains puzzled over this "Garden of Eden" as God's creation. Or perhaps they simply dreamed about how rich it would make the men who might exploit it. Perhaps they contemplated innovative ways to divest the Indians of any claim to that Garden of Eden. How can we possibly know? Absent detailed journal entries, different scenarios are possible. Ambrose opts for portraying the captains as earnest and philosophical. After all, these are more fitting traits for the great men of history than are greed and the view that Indians were hardly more than animals.

In general, Euro-Americans are described in *Undaunted Courage* in glowing and deserving terms. He often characterizes them as heroes and patriots who seek civilizational progress. Most are lovers of freedom who "hate" slavery or at least treat their slaves well. It seems clear from Ambrose's language that his Euro-American characters are proxies for the character of the United States, so deserving of its prosperity in the face of less able European powers:

But there was no hurry, for, as long as Louisiana was in Spanish hands and Ohio River Valley pioneers had access to the wharves of New Orleans, the United States could afford to wait [to explore]. Spain was old and decrepit, growing weaker each year. America was young and dynamic, growing stronger every day. The people who were going to transform the

Mississippi Valley, from its source to New Orleans, into farms and villages would come from the United States, not from Spain.[13]

The above passage leaves little doubt that—like the European powers—Indians (and certainly not slaves) were unfit for this transformation.

In fact, Ambrose is so fixated on white experience that he manages to diminish the overwhelming cruelty and structural economic importance of slavery in one picturesque narrative. He refers to slavery as "a snake" in the "Garden of Eden" of Albemarle County plantations, therefore focusing on the privileged white person's experience of slavery rather than on the slave's experience of slavery. He also writes passages about Indians encountering, welcoming or attacking whites, stealing from or helping, submitting or dying in the periphery of stories that are really about whites. In short, what is written about slaves and American Indians is actually written to explain some situation, characteristic, or quandary of Ambrose's Euro-American subjects:

> But this Garden of Eden was also a potential battlefield populated by numerous Indian tribes containing thousands of warriors. As a result, in addition to being a fabulous field for the botanist and naturalist, the Plains were also a challenging field for the soldier, the peacemaker, the ethnologist and the businessman.[14]

Indian tribes caused Lewis and Clark diplomatic difficulties and thus caused them to order their lives and camps so as not to attract undue and aggressive attention from Indians. Indians were often viewed as deceitful thieves. Many of their behaviors were perplexing to whites. Lewis found Indian women generally unattractive and the peoples generally malodorous. On the other hand, some Natives were considered uneasy friends and helped Lewis and Clark and their men by feeding them, helping them navigate dangerous terrain, giving them other important information, and giving them sexual services.

Ambrose does not balance such perspectives by mentioning that the annals of cross-cultural contact also indicate that Natives have often thought their Euro-American and European colonizers to be malodorous, unattractive, deceitful and perplexing. He also does not speculate about what Natives might have thought of whites encroaching into their homelands. He notes several times that some found Lewis and Clark too meddlesome in inter-tribal affairs. He also mentions that the two were curiously arrogant about their ability to mediate inter-tribal disputes and he reveals Lewis' prejudiced views of Indians. But Ambrose is unconvincing in his attempts to historicize in a way that is critical of white practices. He reveals that his critical lens is not really critical when he emphasizes that whites and Indians were equally ignorant of each other's practices and cultures, as if this were the crucial problem in Indian-white relations. Ambrose thus implies that whites and Natives were equally at fault in their difficult dealings with one another and thus perhaps equally responsible for colonization.

Just as Ambrose consistently centers whites in his history, his tone implies a primarily white audience. Sometimes he pointedly speaks to whites who might imagine themselves as characters in his story:

> In the years following the revolution, life on the Virginia plantation had much to recommend it. There was the reality of political independence. There were the balls and dinners, the entertainment. There was freedom of religion. The political talk, about the nature of man and the role of government, has not been surpassed at any time or any place since. . . Life at Monticello in the years after the revolution was delightful to the eye, ear, taste, and intellect. Just imagine an evening as Thomas Jefferson's guest, following a day of riding magnificent horses over hedges, fields, and rivers, chasing fox or deer or bear...[15]

I can only imagine myself as such an entertained and enlightened guest of Jefferson if I imagine myself as a white, male land-owner. As an American Indian woman hounded all my life by the white-centered story-telling of historians such as Ambrose, I have found liberation in an oppositional practice of reading history. Thus I focus on words such as "independence," "freedom" and "delightful" and ask myself to whom might such words have applied? Would such words have described an Indian's or a slave's experience in regards to Jefferson's plantation? Could they even capture the experiences of most human beings living during the era so grandly described by Ambrose? Ambrose is not speaking to me or about individuals, peoples and events that would resonate with my experience. When Ambrose paints his romantic picture of this free nation, that picture necessarily excludes the experiences of slaves, Indians, poor people and many women.

This brings me back to the post-modernist critique mentioned earlier. While post-modernist perspectives on "History" do not necessarily underlie native critiques, they can join with them to force more space for oppositional Native thinkers both inside and outside academia. For example, philosophers have argued that post-modernism has changed the ways in which we tell or should tell history. Likewise, Native thinkers persistently criticize white men's history as just that, "his story," not ours. Dakota intellectual Elizabeth Cook-Lynn has said that new narratives need to be written of American history as it involves indigenous peoples. In this respect, her voice is one among many in Indian Country. The first such oppositional thinker to inspire me was my mother, LeeAnn TallBear. When I was a student in South Dakota public schools in the 1970s, she gave me anti-colonial histories (both oral and written) to complement school history texts that were sometimes blatantly and sometimes insidiously racist. They were always demeaning of Indian experience.

Cook-Lynn asserts that much of the American history to which we are subjected is "based on the assumptions of a European body of thought which suggests that the American Indian experience is somehow a lesser one."[16] She reminds us of the nation-building work of American literature that is in service to an assumed Euro-American nation. Such literature "claims [sole] possession of the American West" when its authors write about "the plains and the American Indian and their own experiences in an attempt to clarify their own identities."[17] As I have indicated, I level the same critique at Ambrose's retelling of the Lewis and Clark narrative. While Indians and others are integral to the story, their purpose in Ambrose's narrative is to clarify Euro-American national identity and history. In spite of changes in historical scholarship, Ambrose continues with a colonial model of narration in which he tells a story about "discovery" and the "opening" of the West by Euro-American men.

A politically discerning reader might like to read a less nationalistic, more nuanced analysis of Lewis and Clark's journey. James Ronda's *Lewis and Clark Among the Indians* (University of Nebraska Press, 1984 and 2002) is such a book. In many of his more analytical moments, Ambrose cites Ronda. In Ronda's preface he explains what his account offers:

> This book is not a retelling of the familiar Lewis and Clark adventure ... [it] is not an attempt to dress up exploration history in feathers and paint to satisfy current political needs... What this book does offer is something new for the history of exploration in general and Lewis and Clark literature in particular—a full-scale contact study of the official and personal relations between the explorers and the Indians. In 1952, [Lewis and Clark scholar] Bernard DeVoto wrote that "a dismaying amount of our history has been written without regard to the Indians." While much has changed since then, the history of exploration remains largely the story of the explorers themselves.[18]

Indeed, Ronda offers an alternative to Ambrose's account that ultimately reaffirms the flag-waving and romanticized nationalist politics of our day. Ronda offers a historical analysis that better reveals the complicated nature of US history and some of its pivotal characters. He also draws his characters from a more inclusive roster of historical figures. This is no surprise, given that Ronda emphasizes that scholars of history must reckon with their sources. He cautions us not to rely only on the documentation of colonizers (my word) to form historical narratives:

Every historian must first come to terms with his sources. Because the thoughts and actions of men like [the Indians] Weuche, Yelleppit, and Coboway are as central to the story of the expedition as the plans and designs of the explorers themselves, it is important to note the evidence and method used in this study. Despite the kinds of obvious cultural biases that scholars have long since learned to deal with in documentary analysis, the Lewis and Clark records provide a store of information about Indians unequaled in the literature of exploration. When joined to other contemporary evidence . . . the historical record is rich indeed. But by itself that written documentary record cannot fully explain the intricate patterns of encounter that bound Indians and explorers together. To that evidence this study brings the findings of anthropology and archaeology.[19]

By bringing in evidence from other fields, Ronda hopes to give greater "depth and meaning to the behavior of native people" *and* to Lewis and Clark themselves than is evidenced in the standard historical documents. The following passage from Ronda highlights the fundamental problem with the Ambrose account:

As Lewis and Clark were important players with powerful lines, so too were Black Buffalo, Cameahwait, and the Nez Perce woman Watkuweis. If the expedition was what the western photographer Ingvard Edie called it, "the American odyssey," then all the Argonauts—those who ventured to the sea and those who watched in wonder—must have their voices heard.[20]

Ambrose portrays Lewis' experience not as one among other interesting lives in this history, but as somehow definitive of *the* American experience. As I finished reading *Undaunted Courage* I was awed by Ambrose's storytelling ability and by his extensive research. He eagerly told a story to which he obviously felt deeply attached. Unfortunately, his use of language, his characterization, his focus and his style of narration indicate that he took for granted that stories about white men and their accomplishments make "history." Other peoples and their narratives are important chiefly in how they intersect with the experiences of great Euro-Americans. Ambrose's scholarship and writing—whether or not he knew it consciously—reaffirm the notion that the United States is a nation that is primarily for and about white Americans. In 2004, that story still sold well enough to make it a *New York Times* bestseller.

NOTES

[1] Ambrose, 22-3.

[2] Ibid., 471-75

[3] Ibid., 139.

[4] Ambrose laments the fact that because Lewis' journals were so long in being published that he and his men were not given credit for their naming of many natural features. Other explorers who came later re-named them and those names stuck. Given Ambrose's attention to the problems with place naming, I find it amazing that he doesn't mention that many of these places were already named by Native peoples and then again by other Europeans who encountered them prior to Lewis and Clark.

[5] Ibid., 141.

[6] For example, see William Cronon, Ed., *Uncommon Ground: Rethinking the Human Place in Nature* (New York: Norton and Company, 1996).

[7] Ambrose, 108-09.

[8] Ibid., 260.

[9] Ibid., 481.

[10] Ibid., 117.

[11] Ibid., 144.

[12] Ibid., 149.

[13] Ibid., 71-2.

[14] Ibid., 154.

[15] Ibid., 33.

[16] Elizabeth Cook-Lynn, *Why I Can't Read Wallace Stegner and other Essays: A Tribal Voice* (Madison and London: University of Wisconsin Press, 1996), x.

[17] Cook-Lynn, 32.

[18] Ronda, xvii-xviii.

[19] Ibid., xviii.

[20] Ibid., xix.

Where Are They?

Charmaine White Face

There is an old legend of the Titonwan of the Oceti Sakowin. In it, animals desire to kill the first human beings, the two-leggeds, because they fear that the two-leggeds will destroy them and the other relatives on Unci Maka. But the winged ones have pity and want to help the two-legged beings. A great race is held around the Black Hills, more than 500 miles, and the winner will determine the fate of the human beings. The racetrack becomes red with the blood from the hooves, feet, and paws of the animals running the grueling race. But the magpie is smart and rides on a horn of the buffalo, the fastest runner with the most endurance. As they near the end, the magpie, who has conserved his strength, flies ahead of the buffalo and wins the race. As a result, human beings are allowed to live and the buffalo nation must provide for their needs.

In any natural field, one that has not been cultivated by human beings, there might be hundreds of species of plants. Each year, the field will change as seeds grow in relation to the amount of moisture, temperature, and sunlight available the previous winter and spring. But even though this ever-changing living tapestry produces varied kinds of plant life with each new year, there will always be one dominant plant: grass, broad leaf, or perhaps cacti. The less dominant will grow among the more prolific, sometimes in small family clusters, sometimes alone, standing proudly. Perhaps a bird flying overhead has dropped one seed on its way to feed its young, and the seed, left in a favorable position, has grown into a single entity, thus adding a touch of difference to an otherwise homogenous mixture.

Were human beings allowed to co-exist with each other and the rest of creation in certain geographic areas in an environmentally sustainable manner, just such a tapestry would develop over thousands of years. Such was the North American continent when the Europeans invaded. However, such a tapestry was not conceivable for Europeans, after almost 2,000 years of conquest, pillage, and use and abuse of what were known as "natural resources."

When Lewis and Clark traveled along the Missouri River, they were a part of this mindset. They could not know that the indigenous peoples they were encountering had cultures thousands of years old, very complex societal systems, and an understanding of nature that America still does not grasp today. Nor did Lewis and Clark, like the cultures of America or Europe today, realize or understand the indigenous peoples' comprehension of the vast spiritual dimensions of this world.

Lewis and Clark were merely the starter cells of a vast, cancerous way of thinking that is rapidly killing Unci Maka. That thinking started in Europe thousands of years ago. "Natural resources," whether they be oil, minerals, timber or crops, were to be used solely for the production of "things" for the enjoyment and comfort of human beings.

In their journals, Lewis and Clark described the countless numbers and new kinds of species they encountered: the large herds of buffalo drinking at the river, the amazingly graceful antelope and deer lowering their heads to the water in the early evening, the many kinds of waterfowl everywhere. They also expressed the need for interpreters for the many indigenous languages they were encountering, but only for the purpose of trade and business, only for the purpose of conquest and use.

So where are they? Where are the buffalo? Why are they not still running free across the prairies? Where are the black bears, the brown bears, the grizzly bears? Why are they not in the Black Hills? Where are the wolves? They live in family and clan units too. They once lived all over the Midwest. Where are the moose that once traveled in these areas? Where are the mountain sheep that lived so plentifully among the spires and tables in the Badlands?

Where are the plants that were not given Latin names by scientists and botanists but disappeared under plows, or water caused by dams, or were eaten by cattle? Where are the tallgrass prairies? There is a tiny one left in North Dakota, near Fargo, completely surrounded by farms. Yet, at one time, the tallgrasses, taller than a horse, were found all over in the Midwest. How many plants and animals will die, and how many threatened and endangered species will become extinct, so a new railroad line can be built through one of the last pristine grasslands? We are supposed to nevermind that railroad lines are obsolete and only increase air, water, and land pollution. After all, we are told, the railroad cars will carry what is left of the coal in Wyoming to points east. These are parts of the legacy of Lewis and Clark.

Where are the myriad streams of clean water that once flowed in the Black Hills, in the Badlands, all over the prairies, following each spring and summer rain? Where are the flocks of waterfowl that once covered the waterways in South Dakota? A pitiful few have become full-time residents of the location across from the mouth of the Bad River where Lewis and Clark encountered the Titonwan, that place which is now the capitol of the state of South Dakota.

Where are the thousands of trees, shrubs, and bushes that once lined the Missouri River and were the homes, shelter, and food for innumerable animals and birds? Where are the fish and turtles and other small aquatic life that needed the trees and shrubs and bushes to extend their branches over the water so that their breeding places would be shaded from the hot summer sun? Where are the insects that inhabited the trees, shrubs and bushes and were food for some of the water life?

Where is the clean air of the Great Plains? Now it is filled with the noxious fumes of mining for coal and methane and oil. It contains the radioactive particles of hundreds of abandoned uranium mines, particles to be breathed in by humans and cattle, to settle on grass and crops that will be eaten by humans and cattle, and to be carried by the wind elsewhere. These also are part of the legacy of Lewis and Clark.

Where are the Black Hills places that were sacred to the Titonwan and other indigenous nations? Is there a consequence for the destruction of something sacred? How many burial sites containing the remains of the ancestors of the Oceti Sakowin and other tribes have been crushed under cultivators so crops of winter wheat can bring in the almighty dollar? How many sacred places and burial sites, areas that were left in reverence for thousands of years on the prairies, are being considered for destruction so coal can be strip-mined to increase the pollution in the air? How many petroglyphs, places of communication with those wiser than the two-leggeds, have been vandalized with the initials of plunderers, or destroyed by "educated" people to be placed in museums? These are also the legacies of Lewis and Clark.

Where are my people, the Titonwan and the rest of the Oceti Sakowin? Where are the ones of whom Thomas Jefferson said, "On that nation, we wish most particularly to make a friendly impression, because of their immense power..."

Where is the honor of a nation that made treaties with the Oceti Sakowin but then violated them? Where is the integrity of a nation that would go against its own Constitution in order to have access to gold? Where is the humanity of a nation that would steal children to change them from being who the Creator made them to be?

Where are my people of whom William Clark said, "These are the vilest miscreants of the savage race, and must ever remain the pirates of the Missouri, until such measures are pursued, by our government, as will make them feel a dependence on its will for their supply of merchandise?"

Where are the thousands and thousands of Titonwans who perished from starvation, bullets, smallpox and other diseases after Lewis and Clark traveled up the Big Muddy? Where are the Wahpekute, the Wahpetonwan, the Mdewakantonwan, the Sisitonwan, the Ihanktonwan, and the Ihanktonwanna, the other six nations of the Oceti Sakowin?

Where are the children buried who died in residential boarding schools generation after generation? Where are the ones who survived the physical, mental, emotional, and spiritual abuse of the boarding schools and died later of the consequences of their experiences? Where are the burial sites of their parents, the ones who were prisoners of war, who whispered secrets to their grandchildren hoping a miracle would happen and some seed would remain of the Oceti Sakowin?

Where are the ancient family practices of the Oceti Sakowin? Where is the strong societal structure that forbid a son-in-law to talk to his mother-in-law? Where are the whipbearers so that no woman or child had to fear abuse at the hands of a man? Where are the old laws that guided nations for millennia to live and thrive on Unci Maka? These absences are the greatest tragedy of the legacy of Lewis and Clark.

Assigning Meaning to the Lewis and Clark Adventure and the Western Story
Elizabeth Cook-Lynn

Whether you are a serious American historian or a history buff, you know the value of the Diary/Journal, the Photo, and the Fictional Narrative as components of colonial historiography. In the case of the Lewis and Clark history, these genres have produced the logic and context by which America has claimed its roots.

The Diary, such as what was created by Lewis and Clark in 1805, idealizes American maleness; it is the model of the strong intrepid adventurer. Secondly, the Photo, such as the stunning artistic work of George Catlin, promotes "vanishing American Indian" ideology. Thirdly, the Fictional Narratives of a novelist like James Fenimore Cooper present Indians as copycat models for the environmentally sensitive natural American Man.

Using all of this creativity, "real" western historians like Francis Parkman have added the ubiquitous anecdotes so prevalent in pseudo-history, to provide apologia for abandoning the Noble Savage image in favor of the image of the Doomed Indian. Western readers believe in these stories and value this "western" historiography. All of this "colonial literature" is the basis for the political works of the scholars known as the "new historicists."

At first glance, these separate genres seem innocuous, yet when combined with cinema, television or even legislation, they achieve a goal, a young colonizing nation's goal of whitewashing a very ugly history of theft and genocide.

The result has been the cleansing of America. This myth is different from those of other colonizing nations, as it goes about creating its good versus evil themes of the West. The difference, we are told through the Diary/Journal, the Photo, and the Fictional Narrative, is that America has a goodness that other nations usually don't have, that difference being America's Christian origin. In these texts, the Christian God is often called upon and is ever-present at critical times of both grief and joy. The implication is that other colonizing nations have committed atrocities in the name of progress, but that the nation we love, America, has never done so willingly. It suggests that the colonization of this North American continent, inhabited in some areas only by a few ignorant non-Christian "savages," was a benign and inevitable thing; and, most of all, it suggests that Americans are just better than others, that there is a moral purity in being American that does not exist for others.

This mythic vision seems particularly ubiquitous as America celebrates as epic the Lewis and Clark Discovery Journey of two hundred years ago. Myth and history and present experience collide. The journey of Meriwether Lewis and William Clark in the early nineteenth century is the beginning of the western historiography which has permeated all western stories for over two hundred years and now dramatically influences the media, television, radio, Home Box Office and even foreign films. This historiography has been successful in disguising the journey as epic rather than as the colonial invasion for land and supremacy that it really was, the theft of a land possessed by indigenous nations thousands of years old.

To grasp the meaning and pervasiveness of this western mythology, consider an experience I had as a local writer whose work is regionally concerned with politics, the American Indian experience, and scholarship. I was contacted by Kikim Media of Menlo Park, California, to provide a two-minute introduction for a DVD of the HBO series called "Deadwood." I said that I had never seen the series, so they sent some past programs for my viewing.

This story takes place in 1876 in Deadwood, Dakota Territory, some six decades after the Lewis and Clark Journey. Its intent is the examination of the lives of the usual western adventurers such as the intrepid Wild Bill Hickock, the fearless Calamity Jane, the capitalist hotel owner Mr. Farnscheim, several mercantile agents, gold diggers and claims agents, Christian seekers, an eastern investor who is sure to be swindled as he cares for his delicate wife, the prostitute with the heart of gold, the doctor struggling with various moral dilemmas and on and on, all right out of the West as new frontier.

What is remarkable about this newest western story, according to the producers, is the examination of the "corruption" of the people who inhabited Deadwood, yet little of the criminal treatment of tribal people is a part of the plot-making. Absent were such historical realities as these: the settlement of Deadwood was in violation of the Sioux Treaty of Fort Laramie of 1868, for which George Armstrong Custer and his men were killed; the settlement of Deadwood brought about the killing of Crazy Horse, who had been waging a very successful war out of the Powder River, and it was followed by the Congressional theft of the sacred lands of the Sioux, the Black Hills.

Yet this story is, in the view of the producers, a re-imagining, with new insights, a new historicism, and evidence of a new historical consciousness, despite the absence of the history of the evils of colonization and genocide.

I was told that I could say whatever I wanted in my DVD introduction, but it was clear to me that the plot-making was already agreed upon. In response, I suggested that there is nothing new in this story, that the people who inhabited Deadwood in 1876 were no different from the people who inhabit the West even now, that there were then and still are Indian-haters, thieves, liars, swindlers, racists, Christians, aggressive capitalists and stealers of land. What it has all meant to me is that there is nothing new in plot-making.

Perhaps it is useful to examine briefly the intent of four of the earliest sources for this history: the 1804 writings of Lewis and Clark as adventurers (the Diary/Journal), the 1820-30 fictional writings of James Fenimore Cooper known as the Cooper Trilogy (Fictional Narrative), which glorifies the American as the natural man, and the concomitant paintings of disappearing Indians by George Catlin (the Photo). All of these precursors have made it possible for the "Deadwood" series to find its focus, but to suggest that there is something new and revelatory here is wishful thinking.

This historiography does not expose theft of Indian land, brutal colonization, and endemic genocide because the real political abuse of power is often hidden by gunfight-in-the-street violence. One of the failings of the new historicists who make HBO movies is that they do not seem to understand that the real crimes are not in the streets of Deadwood, but, rather, in the broader intent of America to steal a continent by any means possible. Neither do anecdotal historians like Francis Parkman, a storyteller who came along in 1889 and described Indians as Doomed Villains. Doom hangs heavy over the western story as far as Indians are concerned, but there is little expression of the reality of their situation as continuing participants in the region. Greed and strife are obvious, but there is no discourse concerning indigenous powerlessness and its origins. That may be because no one believes that colonizing is an international crime for which human beings must pay.

Often, a description of the genocidal period is intentionally omitted from the overall picture of what America thinks of itself. Historical scholarship, then, omitting the ugliness of colonial invasion, uses the Diary/Journal, the Photo and Fictional Narrative as the "crown jewels" of nation-building in its teaching programs, research, and even contemporary tourism.

This is nothing new in colonial historiography. Indeed, it is a universal phenomenon. Decolonization scholar Professor Ania Loomba, Jawaharlal Nehru University, New Delhi, India is one of the many decolonization researchers of recent years who has made accessible the features of the ideologies of colonial America's historiography. She says "literary texts" (and by that she means the Diary/Journal, the Photo and the Fictional Narrative) are crucial to the formation and support of colonial discourses.

If the Diary/Journal, the Photo, and the Fictional Narrative remain the mainstays of the Lewis and Clark bicentennial sequence, it is reasonable to assume that the sequence will continue to be seen as in some ways another 9/11 nightmare fantasy. In the same way that the Ground Zero people in New York talk today of how "we" are transformed by events, the folks paying attention to the present bicentennial event of two hundred years ago will continue to suggest transformation. The listening world must be offered obsessive flag-waving and endless media hype. Nationalistic obsession is a method of avoidance for those who do not want to be honest about this nation's actions, to avoid the truth: that the American conquest of land deliberately and erroneously described as empty has been a fraud.

In the case of the Lewis and Clark story, we see ordinary quiet and docile American parents and children, grandparents and aunts and uncles, dressing up like pioneers, fur traders, cowboys, wagon train bosses, loose women of the night, gunslingers, steamboat captains, and lost Indians. The message is that the invasion of this continent by European Christians was a good and inevitable thing. As a consequence, the legacy of conquest and colonization, which is now America's hallmark throughout the world, is once again being presented as transcendent freedom.

The real issue is failure of scholarship. Historians who study the Diary/Journal, the Photo, and the Fictional Narrative should be insightful thinkers, not sycophants. Historians, therefore, should resist the Lewis and Clark hoopla and examine what their discipline has wrought, and commit themselves to doing better.

It may be that through an honest examination of the grand expedition of Lewis and Clark, stories and photos and benign reminiscences about America's past and its global "adventures" can be understood as something more than media frenzy and something less then the fantasy of a deserved cultural supremacy in today's world. In that case, perhaps the HBO offering of Deadwood will go the way of all false melodrama. The building of a nation is an imperialistic and violent endeavor in any case, and America is not exempt from this truth. The case against America's contrived history will win out eventually.

From 1804 until 1890, the shaping of a national fantasy and national delirium about it went almost unexamined and the genocidal consequences for indigenous peoples of this continent have been ignored. An honest examination of these consequences might even illuminate America's current imperial behavior toward other nations and peoples in the contemporary world and that would not be a bad thing.

Recently, a writer from the American Indian Museum in Washington, DC, as she was assisting in preparing an exhibit of the works of Catlin for the important Smithsonian commemoration of the bicentenary legacy of that era, telephoned me and posed this question: Aren't Catlin's wonderful pictures of the 1830's and 1840's simply invaluable?" My answer was, "No, of course not!" The question, I reminded her, "presupposes that the genocidal diminishment of the indigenous life pictures in them is simply to be mourned, not examined or analyzed. The Catlin work should be no more celebrated than should the work of all handmaidens of colonialism employed by either military or civil entities."

The period in which Catlin's work was done was called "a century of dishonor" by Helen Hunt Jackson as few decades later, which conflicts with belief in the "wonderfulness" of what Catlin created. It is also important to recognize that nothing said by Jackson or any other dissenters of her period, or of the "new historians" of our time, has put an end to the glorious American fable, even as the legacy of America's imperial behavior plays itself out in Bosnia and Afghanistan and Iraq.

The colonist and imperialist of the nineteenth century treasured the Diary/Journal, the Photo and the Fictional Narrative, but no more than the colonist and imperialist of the present century treasure them. Thus, the work of Meriwether Lewis and William Clark, the literature of imaginative novelists, the pictures of Catlin, and the stories of Francis Parkman become the treasures that burn the American glorious past into the present and future. The Diary/Journal, the Pictures and Fictional Narratives of the modern era contribute to the continued efforts at colonizing the globe in the same way that the Lewis and Clark, Catlin and Parkman works contributed to the colonization of the American continent in the earliest days. They do so because of the failure of scholarship, the failure of historians, the failure of the image-makers to analyze and seek truth.

As these genres go forward, then, unexamined for their self-serving bias, anti-Indian nineteenth and twentieth century legislation goes forward as well. As the Major Crimes Act of 1887 weakened tribal law in early America, the Patriot Act of 2002 tramples on the Constitution and subsumes the rights of all peoples. There is no safe haven when historical truth-telling has been sacrificed.

The ideological thinking concerning early American imperialism in the question asked by the museum curator of Catlin's work can be stated hypothetically: "If you overlook the racism embedded in US history and if you put aside the colonial policies that enslaved dark peoples, both Blacks and Indians, for most of the history of the American past, aren't the works of nineteenth century image-makers invaluable?" After all, the Diaries/Journals by Lewis and Clark are the record of a monumental achievement as well as a drawing of the first 'Map of the West.' Her apparent point is that Catlin's capturing of the beauty of the Indian race is something useful because these people are "vanishing" people and he "treated them with respect," as did Francis Parkman, who moved the description of Indians from the stereotyped Noble Red Man to Doomed Savage. There is something redemptive, then, she probably believes, in these historical genres.

I have never been a believer in such redemption. What needs to happen is this: America, too, needs to refuse to accept the rationale presented in these redemptive strategies of historiography, and when it does, it will be able to think of the original inhabitants of this continent as living and breathing and continuing human inhabitants of the West, neither barbaric nor degenerate, wholly undeserving of the vicious colonial history they have endured. That change and that new scholarship would provide a future for all of us.

Native Reaction

Zion Zetina

So...what does Lewis and Clark mean to me?
Death, disease, turmoil,
Sand Creek and Wounded Knee!
Treaty after broken treaty,
constantly deceiving, destroying, stealing, killing-
does any of THIS ring a bell?
Who else in HELL
could do these things so WELL?
So PARDON ME if I don't CELEBRATE your bicentennial!
If I were Partisan, I would have hijacked the BOAT
and taken every gun and shell!
They took a confused girl, not yet a winyan
named Sakagawea,
and tricked her into guiding-
without HER their chances of surviving
were quickly subsiding
and in hindsight, if she only knew,
she would have left them starving, dying!
But a thriving nation must expand,
murder woman, child and man,
from coast to coast to manifest their cataclysmic destiny plan!
Destruction can only reap destruction-
end of discussion!

That's how I knew
the World Trade Center attacks were coming-
I'm talking of GENOCIDE-
worse than with Ghandi and the Hindus
or what Hitler did to the Jews!
With the Expedition,
Jefferson knew EXACTLY what he was getting into!
He had Lewis taking notes on which tribes
would be easy to colonize!
Oh, but NOT MINE! Certainly, NOT MINE!
Dakotas were on the hit list from the very beginning!
For the simple fact that we were not defenseless-
they detect contention with the tribes that are relentless!
In the history books, they're scared and barely MENTION us!
"Lewis and Clark were 'GREAT EXPLORERS'..."
"Lewis and Clark were 'GREAT EXPLORERS'..."
LEWIS AND CLARK WERE GREAT EXPLOITERS!
Mapping the land and trying to analyze "savage man!"
They say "savage" is insulting-
but if this is CIVILIZED...
I WANT TO BE AS SAVAGE AS I CAN!
...Be as natural as I CAN!
...Be as backwards as I can!
According to the "civilized" standards at hand!
EXPANSION, GLOBALIZATION, INDUSTRIALIZATION!
EXPANSION, GLOBALIZATION, INDUSTRIALIZATION!
cause acidic condensation and DEPLETION
of resources in every NATION!
Modernization leaves your soul vacant and your spirit limited.
That's why for enlightenment, I'm in constant search of the primitive.
So I take the initiative to expose the insidious...
the insidious actions of the fascist imperialist bastards,
cashing in on the masses, creating profitable disasters...
like how the West was lost- or should I say STOLEN?
The Expedition to the Pacific was a specific
step in the process of RAILROADING!

Then the Iron Horse rolled in
with all its motion of commotion
transporting explosives and whiskey potions
with sinister motives.
AND, its all because the President wanted land on both oceans!
Who knows what gave them the notion!
They had NO right!
Then people get surprised and wonder "why?"
when they feel KARMA'S bite!
While decimating His doctrines, they dare to preach the name of
Christ.
It takes a lot of nerve to say, "Jesus loves you,"
during the rape of little girls!
THEY WANT TO RAPE THE WHOLE WORLD-
and take it for what it's worth.
That's why I and my Indigenous people are appointed defenders of the
Earth!
And we do it with no fear militantly or mentally, but never feebly.
So what does the Lewis and Clark Expedition mean to me?
It's a representation of two centuries of battling the Cavalry...
It's a continuation of five centuries of resisting invading armies...
It's a reminder if all the efforts to exterminate Native people over the
years.
And despite their efforts, from the top of Alaska to the bottom of Chile
WE ARE STILL HERE!
Despite all their efforts to exterminate Native people over the years,
From the top of Alaska to the southern tip of Chile,
WE ARE STILL HERE!
WE ARE STILL HERE!
WE ARE STILL HERE!

NOTE
This work was previously published in *Ikce Wicasta*.

Isanti River Journey

Gabrielle Wynde Tateyuskanskan

The living Oyate and ancient rivers
have shared a journey.
The birth of the people began
with pure life-giving water.
A sacred site marked by the confluence
of the gentle Minnesota
and powerful Mississippi Rivers.
This inherited memory has been
etched in my genes.
I am drawn to rivers.
They are sanctuaries for my spirit.

Respect for the river's heart has sustained
the Oyate for many generations.
Dakota ancestors have often traveled
the natural highways created by water.
Sisitonwan have been supported by
the bounty water has provided.

They are the dwellers of the fishing villages.
In the eyes of the tiyospaye
there is a familial understanding
of place that words cannot express.
I am never alone on the
cool, clear, shimmering water.

In 1600 a malignancy
appeared on the waterways.
Disguised as humankind
it slowly and secretly began to
corrode the natural world.
Traveling against the current, it concealed
itself in kinship to the tiwahe.

During the fall of 1862
the Minnesota River Valley was chilled by
the unfulfilled promise of treaty annuities.
Starving Dakota women and children were
force-marched from Cansayapi
to a concentration camp
located near the precious
river womb of origin.

During the spring of 1863 imperiled Isanti
elderly, women and children
began a river journey of deportation.
Imprisoned on an overcrowded steamboat
taken by an undertow of sorrow
to the convergence of the
Mississippi and Missouri Rivers.

Moving against the Missouri River current
the vulnerable prisoners
were taken to Fort Thompson
on the arid plains.
Here the invading cancer mercilessly
drowned the helpless Oyate
in the dust of the parched plains.
Many took refuge in the spirit world.

Humanity stood silent to
the destruction of Dakota homelands,
culture, language, spirituality and families.
Moral discomfort was soothed by
"Manifest Destiny."

Many beloved Dakota relatives
disappeared during this forced removal.
In spite of their pained and weary hearts
the surviving prisoners had the
courage and strength to dream a future.
Tears became a prayer song of hope for the Oyate.

In 1867 the Sisseton and Wahpeton
moved back to Lake Traverse and were
reunited with their ancient waterway.
The people will never forget that
they were prevented from
grieving ceremonially for their losses.

During 1991 the remains
of some Dakota war casualties
were repatriated and buried.
The Dakota Oyate walked with anguished hearts
in November 2002 to remember
ancestors who disappeared.

Like ancient rivers that have
reshaped their shores
the people have adapted,
moving from loss toward life.
An attentive heart knows a river's well-being
is a measure of our humanity.

I am inspired by the enduring wisdom and
beauty of water.
I have an understanding of the power
of a river's spirit
to give life as well as tears.

In dreams I share memories
of ancestors held in my veins.
Their whisper of hope is carried
by the healing sound of water.
Mni Wiconi
Water is life.

A Nickel for Your Thoughts
Joel Waters

*In response to the new US nickel commemorating the
bicentennial of the Lewis and Clark expedition*

a nickel for your thoughts
but no more valuable
as america has made its racist
views of indians rhetorical
by making a more efficient
peaceful nickel

like saying "oh forget the atrocities"
we have covered it up
by showing symbols of peace
but what of the greed of the BIA
or the broken treaties
is all that just supposed to go MIA?
it's a new backside lie
coming from the same old face

all to remember lewis and clark
and people are in discussion
about building a theme park
over stolen land
and we could all pretend
they're the new
micky mouse and donald duck
just pave over the past
to make a quick buck

there are two sides
to every war story
but the shiniest upside is shown
for all its cheap glory

cheap like our land
that was sold at four pennies an acre
but no indian was there that day
as whitemen sold to whitemen
making convenient policy makers

because back then
and maybe even now
indians were never seen as being equal
to the white people
just a copper penny
next to a shiny nickel

what would you do
if someone put a price tag on your home
and sold it with no remorse?
this country became
one big wholesale store
and it never closes
because there's always something to buy
and something to sell
and pretty soon
no one will be able to tell
...what truth really is

here's a nickel for your thoughts

Reflections on Mnisose after Lewis and Clark
Kathryn Akipa, Gladys Hawk, Craig Howe, Lanniko Lee,
Kim TallBear, and Lydia Whirlwind Soldier

A Dialogue between members of the Oak Lake Writers' Society held at The
Birdsong Inn and Guest House, Java, South Dakota,
February 12, 2005

Kim TallBear In this collection of essays, we have decided to center the river as an actor, and not simply think of it as a subject or something simply acted upon in our response to Lewis and Clark. So, we—Craig and I —want to have you all philosophize about rivers as entities or beings in themselves. It's kind of an open question where you might talk about the meaning of the river to you personally, to your family, to your tribe.

Lanniko Lee All my life I have known the river to be part of a larger expression of our relationship to everything that is—everything that exists. A good example is what Arvol Looking Horse[1] published in his wonderful "World Peace and Prayer Day." In it he describes the earth as a living organism having anatomical functions similar to that of the human body. Mnisose, the river we know, is a major artery. As a major artery it is meant to flow for the life of the world.

In fact, long before scientists began speculating about the alleged benefits of changing the river, my family, like Arvol, talked about the river as doing the work of circulation. Circulation is the vital function of the Mnisose. After all, flowing water brings necessary changes. So when I think about the man-made dams that obstruct the river's flow, I can't help but grieve over the loss of a river flowing and the loss of its life-giving and healing forces coursing through Unci Maka, Grandmother Earth, to the ocean.

Another important conversation for indigenous people regarding caring for the earth is the ability of the rain forest to continue functioning in a healthy way. So much destruction of the rain forest is occurring. Soon it will not be able to do what it was meant to do—provide the essential respiratory exchange needed to keep body Earth healthy. Arvol's message was a proposal to all humanity that we pay attention to how the relationships of the parts of the world work and how we are all responsible for Earth's health. This is good Lakota reasoning.

I remember the elders of my family asking how the clouds would be able to come if there were no trees to call in the clouds. This was after hearing John F. Kennedy's speech about the progress and the good that would come after the river was dammed and hydroelectric power would be available to improve the lives of everyone. My recollection of those times is a mixture of strong emotions interfused with memories of ceremonies and dire prophecies; photographs were taken by those who wanted to remember a river that was destined to be changed. Strong emotions were displayed; everyone living along the river was affected by those changes.

Kim Gladys and Lydia and Kathryn have also talked a lot about the effects on the people and also what the river meant to them personally. How do each of you feel about the Missouri River project and the inherent contradiction for Native people of referring to the River as a "project"?

Lanniko When I grew up, the river was at the center of conversations about the sacred. The river helps explain our belief about the sacred permeating our lives. Images of baptismals are prominent in my memory. All of the songs that we sing when we are burying our people who have grown up along the river are always focused on the water. Gladys can probably talk about that.

Gladys Hawk My piece in this anthology is my personal experience of the river. But it was the Grand River I was talking about. It wasn't far from the Missouri, though. I am also familiar with the Missouri just traveling back and forth to Mobridge. I write about a time when all of the river was still there, but it was being planned to be flooded. I remember seeing the surveyors when they came along the hillside right above our house; they were way up there, so I rode on my horse and I went up there and I asked them, "What are you doing?" There were two guys there with their tripods and they said, "Well, some day the water level is going to be this high" [gestures]. I looked at that and I looked down towards our house and to the river and to the east. I couldn't imagine it; I just could not imagine that. But that was when I was only about ten. And it wasn't until '58, '59 and '60, when I was in my twenties, when we actually saw it happen, when they cut down all the trees along the river and it was bare.

Kim Some of us here were talking last night in the kitchen about the sense of disbelief that people had. First of all, that morally the Army Corps could do this and second, that technologically it was possible. And I wonder if, because it took so long from planning to the actual flood, the sense of disbelief was really big? Or did people gradually accept it would happen?

Gladys I think they gradually accepted it. What more could they do? Their homes were taken away. I just want to say the impact that it had. There was an old man that lived where the bay is now. His name was Ed Hawk. He was an old man with a blind eye. All he had was just two little sorrel horses that he used for his wagon. He had them in the corral and one little log cabin where they wintered. And he lived in a one-room log house. He would not sign anything that the Corps brought in. He just stood his ground. And the Corps came in and they bulldozed his little house. [One gasp of disbelief, then 30 seconds of silence.]

Lydia The damming of the river displaced a lot of people and multiple generations from the river. It destroyed a way of life that was centuries old. I remember somebody telling me that their grandparents would go to the river every Sunday and sit on the bluffs overlooking the water just to see their land disappearing under the water. They would reminisce about the old days, their gardens, their livestock and their homes. And they would feel sad over how their lives had changed since their land was flooded.

As a Sicangu, I didn't grow up along the river. But when they started building the dam near Pierre, my dad worked on it for one summer. He was really torn about that, but he had to support a family. So he just worked on it one summer and then found work elsewhere. But I remember every summer my grandparents would take us to the river by Pickstown, Fort Randall, to see how far the water had come up. We would spend the day, go to Fort Randall and have a picnic and they would sit and talk about the river. They were in disbelief that this could be done. But I was a little kid and as a little kid you don't pay too much attention. As Sicangus we lived so many hours away from the river, but we still went to the river to see what was happening every summer.

Lanniko Another arrogant, irresponsible act occurred even before politicians set in motion those changes to the river. Locals took it upon themselves to move prayer stones off the river—very large boulders that had previously been prairie altars where mortals communed with the sacred. If you go down the river road here, you will see those prayer stones with hand marks on them made during prayer—prayers that were given for that river. One such group, not American Indians, decided to construct a building in Gettysburg, South Dakota; a big prayer stone was moved in to attract tourists to the community. Now if you want to visit one of these stones, you can visit the Dakota Sunset Museum and pay a fee to see the prayer stone, but not to touch it, nor do you have the open, private prairie setting to use the stone as it had been used for hundreds, possibly thousands of years. By moving those stones off the river—it's like another group of people is shaping even our memory. Between that and the river project, maybe they were thinking we would forget our past. Those who were involved in making the decisions to change the river—they knew what they were doing culturally and economically to our lives. I don't know how they can possibly be unaware of what they were doing.

Kim Kathryn, in your essay, you talked about your mom getting a new teaching appointment in Iowa and leaving Lower Brule. Did you actually see what happened after the flooding or did you leave before it got flooded?

Kathryn We left before it got flooded. But a couple of girls who my mom taught came with us on the move. And then when we took them back we heard the stories, the horrible things that happened with the flood. At the store the people would talk around the stove and they would sit there smoking and they just couldn't believe it. "How could they do something like this? How is this possible?" They would ask. The underlying feeling that I remember as a child when I was probably about eight was "How could man think that he is so powerful that he could change the course of the river?" And I remember that there was almost a feeling of toksta. They are going to find out the river will take its own course eventually and it will come back on them. You can't change the course of something like that—so powerful—so mighty. Somewhere you're going to pay for it. That was the feeling of disbelief that the people around the stove and the women in their sewing circles had. It just seemed like such an absurd and far-fetched plan. How could the wasicu think like this?

It reminds me of when they decided to go to the moon in the later 60s—the same kind of idea—a kind of disbelief! [laughter]. But the dam in particular worried a lot of people because a lot of them could not afford to move the graves and they worried about their relatives. Sure enough, three weeks after the flooding they saw caskets floating down the river. That flabbergasted people in the Lower Brule area. Out of respect, I didn't want to put that scene in my essay. It could hurt people to be reminded of that. Some of them, those were their relatives.[2]

I remember such disbelief from my child's point of view. I didn't fully understand the whole thing. I just knew that a flood was coming and that the village would be gone—everything that we knew there. And I think that is the reason why I wrote in my piece about the happy memories as a child, to show the tragic loss. My point was to show that this is on the continuum of what began when Lewis and Clark sailed—the so-called progress of America and how it continues to impact Native Americans in modern times. When you lose a village where you did have such good memories—yes, some of them were tragic and life goes on—but when you lose a village like that and you know that you will never be able to walk in those places again because they're under water, it's hard to imagine.

Kim You just stated clearly the importance of the dam in the legacy of American progress. Lewis and Clark were also part of that movement towards "progress." I'm also interested in what you all have to say about the need to respect the river, its power, and the possible consequences of not respecting it.

Lydia I grew up listening to old people and their philosophies. One of the phrases that they always used was "mni wiconi," which means "water is life." It also means respect for water—respect for river. As long as you have water, there is life. The old people use that phrase in their prayers and everyday conversation.

Lanniko Vine Deloria and Dan Wildcat in their book, *Power and Place*, have also talked about Indian peoples' respect for the river.[3] They talk about our understanding of the changing nature of the river, our understanding of flood plains, of the appropriate places for habitation, and what kinds of things people did to fit their own lives into the balance by understanding the river's changes. They state that with that knowledge, people were able to take care of themselves, while non-Indians build on the flood plains with a lot of investment and insurance. They make money off tragedies that they participate in creating. A critique of capitalism comes across in their book—a conversation about non-Natives who build on the flood plains and reap benefits from loss. They say we never did that because we had a responsibility for not just ourselves, but our whole family—for those communities along the river. We had to have a sense of our responsibility as humans, an understanding of the river phenomena and its changing nature. We had to respect it so that we could share that wisdom with those around us.

Let me give a couple of specific examples of how understanding and respecting the river translated into taking care of our families and communities. We sang songs when we were burying our family members who had grown up and died along the river. We focused on the power of the water, both the sacred power and the power expressed in the cycles of nature. Each spring—as our elders taught us—the seasonal power expressed in floods brought about the renewal of the landscape, of life.

I have another example of how we linked river knowledge and river power to the knowledge and power in our human lives. Late one summer evening when my grandmother and I were down at the river getting water, a light breeze started the cottonwood leaves chattering overhead; she told me to stop and listen. A sliver of moon hung in the sky and she motioned up to it and then to the trees: "Listen to the cottonwood women talking," she said to me. I asked her what they were saying and she said that I should always remember that I am like the river and that one day I would flow and become a woman. Like the popping trees in the spring, and later when the ice was breaking, I would live a springtime, like the river, and bring life into the world. It was then that I learned about how the seeds of cottonwood trees are imbedded into the soft river soil by the swift moving waters that flooding causes in the spring run-off. I learned about the gift of life, and she made clear to me the Lakota saying, "Our children are sacred," with her explanation of how young cottonwood trees were the gifts of floods. I learned then to respect those powerful changes and appreciate our connection to the river, the trees, and the land.

Our everyday lives were spent learning lessons about change and our people used those lessons to make decisions like where to build our homes and where to plant our gardens. Immigrants have not learned much from American Indians when it comes to human connectedness to the land. Our understanding of home is probably because we know Earth as our grandmother, Unci Maka. Unfortunately, our perspective and the wisdom of our elders are never fully appreciated, especially when it comes to stewardship, or when environmental changes are contemplated.

To go back to your comment about disbelief, I think it is untrue that indigenous people had no real sense of the power of technology. On the contrary, our people were more keenly aware of the power of making choices. It wasn't that we all disbelieved that the river's course could be changed. We were in disbelief that the wasicu would do such a thing. Our choices as Lakota people were made from a different way of discerning the world.

Kathryn I just want to make a comment about the Dakota world. Although I lived along this river as a child, we Dakota don't in general live that close to the river. Of course we do have the Mississippi, the Yellow Medicine, the Great Sioux, the Minnesota. . . a lot of rivers. The water was always a very big part of our lives too. It's like you say, Lydia, mni wiconi.

My father, my step-dad, Woodrow Keeble, was born in 1917. His dad was Isaac Keeble, who was very traditional, and never learned to speak a wasicu language. My step-dad used to tell us how to get up in the morning. The old way of making your day is to go out on your own to the east. You face the sunrise and when the sun breaks, you acknowledge the creator, "Wakan Tanka Tukansina." You acknowledge the day and the gift of life that you have and the woods and everything around you on every horizon. That is one of the important things that they did in those days when we lived in camps—we always camped by some kind of water. You would go down in that sacred moment of silence early in the morning to greet the creator, to wash your face, or to use the water in some way to bless yourself. Because it is mni wiconi.

My dad used to tell about how when he was a little boy, his dad would tell them, all six of them, all boys, "Inajin po," and they would get up. They lived on the west side of Pickerel Lake and they would all have to run down to the lake and he would make them jump in the water. They would all have to go in for a swim in the morning, until the ice formed and they couldn't get through the ice any more. And if the little ones tried to complain, he would tell them that it makes your heart strong. And it made my dad's heart strong. He was North Dakota's most decorated war hero from World War II and Korea. He was never given the medal of honor that he was recommended for three times because it was a racial issue—and that's been acknowledged now. But that's just an aside—a plug for my dad! [Laughter]. He lived when it was important to greet your day with the water and to face the sun and commune with Wakan Tanka.

Kim I grew up in Flandreau [SD] mostly, always living about a half mile from the Big Sioux River. Every time I go by a river—it doesn't matter if it's that one or another one—I always look down and think, "I wonder where that goes?" It's always struck me that rivers are roads, yet I haven't spent a lot of time on rivers, canoeing or anything. But I've always felt that they are going somewhere, going somewhere in a good way. I've always been interested in what's at the other end. I don't know if I focused on rivers as travel routes because I always wanted to go somewhere ever since I was small, to travel and see other places, or because there is something in my cultural memory—I don't know how to describe it—in which rivers were our roads. And I think rivers are still central to the Dakota landscape today.

Lydia Rivers were important boundaries for us. In land descriptions, in maps, in designating meeting places, a river would be mentioned. We had Lakota names for all of the rivers in our territory. The Mnisose was the grandfather river. The course of the river can be changed, but how does the change affect the environment? How does that change affect the lives of the people, the animal and plant nations? These were not issues that the government thought about when it built the dams. How many of those animals and plants that Lewis and Clark saw are now extinct? And, how many more will disappear? Can man ever replace what was lost?

Lanniko Last spring I went down to St. Louis and traveled back up the river during spring break. I went along the road coming up and I made a point of going off the road and I saw those levees, big mounds directing water up away from the river, and it reminded me of a picture from when I went to parochial school. We learned all about how the great gardens of the world in the Christian belief were created, how they were all built by slave labor. The whole idea was to turn the desert into the Garden of Eden. When I came up the river from St. Louis, I was reminded of all of that human energy needed to reshape the landscape, and how the newcomers didn't call us people of the river. Yet that's where we were *always*. We were instead called people of the plains.

And it became a self-fulfilling prophecy, that label, one that reminds us of what has been taken away from us. Whether it's the Big Sioux or the Grand or the Cheyenne, we were people of the rivers. Yet now some of our own people don't have an understanding of what the river is. Especially young people have no real understanding of that history. Many of them grew up away from the river, moved off the river to Eagle Butte and live on the Cheyenne River Reservation. They have very little understanding of the cottonwood stories, the fish stories. They don't interact with the landscape—which they can hardly do when they're in the [boarding school] dormitory or with parents or relatives who are caught up in BIA employment or tribal employment or they're in the churches—when they're part of the institutions that shape them with western thinking. They don't have the same kind of connection with the landscape which in itself is the primal, sacred language of the very being of indigenous people.

When Lewis and Clark came up, I can't help but think that with all their litany of what they saw, the things they described in their journals, that they were thinking in terms similar to the Garden of Eden. And the plant life and birds and animals were there waiting for them to catalogue as new species, to re-name. They were coming from a Christian philosophy of understanding, of what happened in another part of the world. To name and catalogue—to try to know everything—is a way that is opposite to the way we had. We didn't go about naming objects, plants and phenomenon like Western explorers; our belief back then was that the "thing" gave its power and the knowledge of its being-ness to us. We didn't have names for everything because not everything gave us its name. The landscape is loaded with mysteries.

Certain plants gave us the power to heal when we used them and they gave us their names. Such knowledge came to those who made it their work to help others through healing. Those people were taught how to work with those things; they received that knowledge through dreams and the like. Today, people who hold such knowledge have also learned that it is not valued like scientific knowledge. We don't talk about those things today. Instead, our people give up that powerful knowledge to be treated by Indian Health Service and Western medical practitioners.

Kim Your comments bring to mind one of my pet peeves. I used to do environmental program planning for tribes and I don't like when people so often say that we are inherently environmentalists—that it's in our blood. Because I think that discounts the fact that we got knowledge of our landscape by interacting with it and having a relationship with it. We—or our ancestors—learned those things and cultivated that knowledge; they weren't just born with it. It's about practice. And if you don't acknowledge that, then you don't necessarily have to practice. So you lose a lot of knowledge by not using those resources every day like in the past and then having a thoughtful spiritual relationship with them.

But I was also interested in something else you said, Lanniko. Were you relating Lewis and Clark's classification of species to cultivating a landscape or creating a certain kind of landscape?

Lanniko The Christian heritage they inherited— Jefferson, Lewis and Clark— has a certain understanding of the Middle East and how the Middle East deserts were manipulated to be habitations for large numbers of people. So when we talk about large populations of outsiders coming into this country, what better way to accommodate them than to harness ideas— with roots in Middle East history—to build the nation and to overcome the landscape that was here to accommodate the European? That was what I was referring to when I said that there was a design. And that design is still evident along that path that I drove to St. Louis and back. There are long mounds that were created to hold the water, to pull that water farther away from the channel of the river in order to create farms. But now all the cities are choked with big plumes—pollution emissions in the air and effluents in the water. They've harnessed the power of the river but that power has another objective now. Rather than being gardens, it is trapped by industries.

I think that with the advancing technology, the vision that was there has changed. I can't help but imagine that in the abundance of what Lewis and Clark saw, they must have felt they had fallen into some wonderful magical place. Whatever they saw when they were out there with their surveyors and looking at the raw, innocent landscape, seeing what potential was there—I would be very curious to see what they saw for the future of that landscape. What did they anticipate they would achieve?

Kim Craig, do you want to talk a little about your perspectives about what the intentions of Lewis and Clark were? We've had some debate amongst ourselves—more in the pieces we've written than in spoken conversation—about what the intentions and goals of Lewis and Clark and the Corps of Discovery were. For example, in terms of Lewis and Clark's classification of species, Lanniko made an interesting point in relating the classification to the eventual taming of the landscape. It's not a direct connection perhaps in terms of their goals, but can be seen as part of an overall vision.

Craig Howe Theirs was a scientific expedition. Jefferson charged them with recording all of those things that were new to science. It was not new to humanity. It was old knowledge to all of those Indian tribes. Lewis and Clark were documenting it for scientific purposes, so it was a new "discovery" for them. At most, in terms of future settlement, they were thinking about how to get trading posts up here. The records do not seem to support that they were considering that non-Lakotas or non-Indians would be living up here in vast numbers. It is hard for us to imagine, but at that time they couldn't see the US population exploding, I don't think. They were not that visionary. Jefferson himself thought it would take hundreds of years before non-Indians would get here. So the idea was not to be negative but to be good to Indian tribes because there was no way they could alone extract the resources of the area. There were too few Americans, so they had to try to figure out a way to use the Indians to exploit the natural resources while simultaneously making Indians dependent upon the US.

In the bigger picture today, I think we put a lot more emphasis on Lewis and Clark; we make them into a bigger event than they were. Because the non-Indians are celebrating the bicentennial of Lewis and Clark we too put too much emphasis on it. Lewis and Clark didn't *cause* anything in my mind. They came and they left.

Lydia It was the beginning of the end of the Mnisose, the beginning of the end to a way of life as our people knew it.

Craig The fact is that there were non-Indians here for decades before Lewis and Clark came.

Lydia But before them it wasn't a scientific expedition to record rivers and tribes and start counting Indians. The Europeans who came before them learned to live with the Natives. Lewis and Clark had a purpose to record what would be in their way when they did finally come. They were a scouting party. They learned that the Lakotas are a fierce tribe that they'd have to deal with. They were probably the first grave robbers to enter Lakota territory.

Lanniko I don't think we can speak of Lewis and Clark without speaking of Jefferson. He was a visionary individual. Anybody can *talk* about empire-building, but he had so many projects ongoing in different aspects of his personal life. And being the public man that he was, some of those projects spilled over into the public realm and this one was one of them.

Kim I just read something about Jefferson being essentially the first American archaeologist in that he started excavating the mounds on his property. Today, we all know about that method of scientific inquiry, but at that time, trying to decipher human history through examining human bones was not something people did. It was a very weird thing to go dig up bones and study them. So it is argued that he was very much a scientist in his own right.

But this brings me back to the idea that rather than Lewis and Clark's individual intentions or even those of Jefferson, what's more important is what that journey has come to symbolize for people. That's why Kathryn's point is interesting—that they were part of another continuum, not necessarily that they directly impacted something but that they were part of a broader cultural movement that resulted in the kinds of things that you're talking about in your pieces about the taming of rivers. But that also gets back to Craig's point too: You don't have to attribute to them intention or necessarily direct responsibility for these things. But certainly I would view them as part of American westward expansionism because science is part of that. Science was very much a tool of expansionism.

Craig Yes, science also involves "discovery." Another kind of wanting to be the first . .

Lanniko Politics too. You don't want to forget that. You can't practice science without practicing politics.

Kim It was one of Jefferson's big political tools, right? Science.

Lanniko Yes. To me that's just another language for being able to be intrusive. The whole business of excavating is the story of European expansion and control.

Craig What Jefferson was trying to do was give the fledgling United States a "History." In Europe they had the castles and ruins, and so what he was trying to do when he wrote a paper about this was to show that over here there was a history. He also wanted to show how things were even bigger over here than in Europe. So he was looking for these mastodon bones. . .

Kim Yes, Jefferson and others were having fights with French naturalists who said "Oh, *nothing* has happened over there." So, if you know that he was fighting with French naturalists and trying to prove that there was history here worth talking about . . .

Craig Right! So he used American Indians to show them how much better this continent was. "Look, American Indians are taller and stronger and did more than you Europeans and your ancestors." Jefferson, on that level, was promoting the noble savage. He was promoting a sense of indigenousness here. Later, maybe he argued another side, but at that time he was trying to give the US an identity separate from Europe. And he argued, "What does the US have that Europe doesn't? It has this indigenous history, it has American Indians and it has the landscapes and the species that are unique here—that you do not have over in Europe and so that's what makes this new country strong." That is what would give this country a unique identity.

Kim I see that as an early sign of Euro-Americans trying to become indigenous here.

Craig And that's why when they dressed up at the Boston Tea Party, they didn't dress up as colonists. They dressed up as Mohawks. The whole idea was to take on the identity of the land so they became Indians in order to fight against the British.

Kim So why are Lewis and Clark so important now? Is it just because we all the feel the need to respond to the commemoration? I certainly never thought about them before the bicentennial very much. I remember knowing who they were—we probably all heard about them in school. But have others of you thought about them extensively and the repercussions of what they did?

Lanniko Not me. But I realize that the bicentennial event is an attempt to rejuvenate a sense of belonging here. People are all capitalizing on an historical event in order to have some prominence here today. There are squabbles all up and down the river about how to sell the bicentennial. Although more recently there has been more positive language. I just heard on public radio about the indigenous perspective, indigenous commemorations. But that also seems like another effort to try to bring capitalist enterprise to this part of the world. As Americans we've exhausted everything; we've wasted and exhausted so much that we're now looking at capitalizing on history to get the world to come and see and spend their money here.

Kim It sounds like you're talking not only about whites but about indigenous people too.

Lanniko Yes! Absolutely! It's cultural enterprise—cultural tourism that they're hoping to achieve, not only whites but Indians too. They're talking about the positive financial repercussions of the Lewis and Clark commemoration today as a result of people coming to this part of the world to see who we are . . .

Kim Craig was saying in an earlier meeting that the Lewis and Clark centennial in 1904 was not such a big deal, right?

Craig Right.

Kim So, Lewis and Clark have in fact been revitalized as historical figures. In 1904, most Americans didn't know who they were.

Craig Yeah, it wouldn't even be close to how it is now.

Lydia Now, they're creating American heroes for their own history books.

Kathryn I didn't really think about them before this commemoration. In school, yes, they were some more wasicu people I had to learn about. But when I was a kid, the only thing that was interesting about them—in depictions of them—they kind of looked more like us. I thought, "How come they wear clothes like that?" They weren't going around with the little powdered wigs and the fluffy blouses. They looked more like real people—the way they were dressed. But they were still wasicus. I never really gave it too much thought. My thing as a kid was trying to keep them all straight. I had to keep all these American heroes straight in my mind and I didn't really make too much effort to do that [laughs].

Lydia They also took Indians and created Indian heroes for their own history —those Indians who helped white people. When you're a little kid trying to hang on to your identity and your cultural pride and you see those Indians who helped the whites destroy our way of life, like Sacajawea, you began to wonder why people cannot accept and appreciate differences. If we don't conform, we cannot be successful in the eyes of the whites.

Gladys Who interpreted that name? I always ask that because I'm curious. Apparently in 1904 they must have had a dedication in Mobridge because my oldest sister had a picture of my grandfather and my grandmother—they were young then—standing near a monument to Sacajawea just across the river from Mobridge. There was a chain fence around it and all of our relatives were standing there. The women had on shawls, of course. I thought "that must have been an important day." They must have dedicated that monument that day. My grandparents, they said "Zintkala Winyan."

Lydia What?! Oh, I always thought "wea" in Sacajawea sounded like "woman" [referring to winyan, the L/D/Nakota the word for "woman"]. Zintkala Winyan, oh, Bird Woman.

Gladys Zintkala Winyan, that's how they talked about her and it means Bird Woman.

Lydia Now that makes sense! I always wondered about that name. In Lakota "saca" means, something brittle and hard. Some people were even pronouncing it "Sacacawea." You know what "caca" means so that couldn't be right.

Gladys I was wondering if "Sacajawea" was a spin-off of "Zintkala Winyan," that the wasicus couldn't pronounce it. I wondered if that was the best that they could do and now we know her as Sacajawea.

Kathryn Is that what it means in her language?

Craig She had two names. One is Shoshone and one is Hidatsa. And one of them, I think, means Bird Woman. But it would have been strange if she had a Lakota name because Lakotas never saw her. She was never on this stretch of the river.

Gladys But I heard them talking about her where I grew up, "Zintkala Winyan." She was known. I never heard of Lewis and Clark, but people talked about *her*.

Craig I can't remember hearing about Lewis and Clark at school.

Lydia I remember seeing pictures, the explorers standing in canoes and pointing toward the west and wearing buckskin clothing like real frontiersmen.

Kathryn This whole bicentennial has forced me to look at it. Of course, as an adult you have a different view when you know the history that has ensued.

Lanniko When I was a girl, I somehow got it fixed in my head that Sacajawea was a barren woman. "Saca, saca," which in Lakota means dry or shriveled up, like someone's hands when they have been in water a long time. And then "wea," which sounds like "winyan", and I put that together to mean *dry woman*. That's what got stuck in my head [laughter]. I was a child interpreting "Who was this woman? She couldn't have children from a man of her own people." I had this really wild imagination! I thought she could only have a child with a wasicu, a Frenchman. She had Little Pompy.[4]

Kim Do you think she is more important to non-Indians then to Indians, because we don't talk about her that much?

Craig Sacajawea makes the Voyage of Discovery a great story because then it's a multi-gender and multi-cultural story. That's why it resonates with people so strongly.

Lanniko That's the reason that we created the Unity Fest and the Sacajawea Learning Center in Mobridge [SD]. The reason why we did it there is because people from other places in the world know about Mobridge because of the brutalities that have been publicized all over the world in newspapers. So when strangers come through the door who have that knowledge, some of them do ask questions and I refer them to our efforts to try to change that history with the Unity Fest, to learn about one another and hopefully have some better understanding of our human-ness, our frailties and also our capabilities to relate to each other in a positive way.

Craig I think again that if we look at the historical documents, none of the Winter Counts mention Lewis and Clark. So if we use that as a milestone, was this event that important? Little Big Horn is so important to non-Indians. It's the most written-about battle. And Lewis and Clark are so important to non-Indians. But again, using the Winter Counts as evidence, Lewis and Clark are not that important.

Lydia It's not that Little Big Horn was not an important event to us, but that people were afraid to talk about it because they were afraid of retaliation. It couldn't be put in a winter count because then it could be taken as evidence against those involved. Bad enough the 7th Cavalry took revenge against Big Foot and his band at Wounded Knee.

Kim Kiowa writer N. Scott Momaday has stated that "Lewis and Clark remains in my mind one of the great epic odysseys in American history." So what's your interpretation of such a perspective?

Lydia For the Americans it is [an epic odyssey] in their history, but I don't see it that way.

Craig I think in human history it is an epic odyssey. We have to go beyond "the" Indian viewpoint as if there is a single Indian viewpoint and we have to judge Lewis and Clark on where they fit in the big picture of human history. At that time and in this place they tried to do something that they thought was really, really important. It was against a lot of odds that they fulfilled their mission, although they failed in the main thing they went to look for—that [water] passage to the Pacific. And they had to realize that failure early and yet they soldiered on. In lots of ways, they brought all types of new knowledge back. They were outdated by the time they got back. To me, that's the important point—that they didn't *cause* anything. By the time they got back, they were meeting non-Indians going up the river. You can read the journals; all the way down, they were meeting non-Indians coming up the river. They weren't the first. All these peoples along this stretch of the river had seen non-Indians before.

Kim I think that's how "the" history books are portraying them, as being the first.

Craig And a lot of us buy into that. Lewis and Clark wanted to be the first—that was their whole goal. And by us perpetuating the idea that they were the first, they're winning in a sense—we're still bought into their incorrect history. They weren't the first—they weren't even close to the first. They weren't that important as individuals. But that journey, as a journey, was on this almost epic scale in terms of the importance it has had to this nation. The truthfulness of these epic journeys is a whole different issue. But a lot of nations have these epic journeys and we can have that in the migration stories of Native tribes. This was the epic journey for this nation.

Kim So, it's more the way the story is told than perhaps what actually happened?

Craig And I think the great thing for us, the great opportunity we have, is that it's in historical time and we have the documents so that we don't have to treat it as myth. We can come back and interrogate it. And we can challenge that epic journey of this nation. And we can challenge it using the technologies and the techniques of that nation. And I think we have abundant evidence to challenge that—the truth value of that epic journey.

Kim I don't mean to pick on Momaday, because it's important to know the context in which he made his statement. But while one might truthfully make that statement, as a Native person I would never say that without also saying "and this is what it means to us—it doesn't mean the same thing to us." Liz [Elizabeth Cook-Lynn, a founding member of the Oak Lake Writers] has also pointed out that he said he was in awe of the Lewis and Clark journey.

Craig I can see it! If you sent 40 guys with the knowledge they had at that time, to do all that, it's awe-inspiring at some level. I'm awed by the fact they were able to do it. Now, that doesn't mean that I think it's an awesome thing, right? I'm awed by the fact that they decided they would do that. How it's played out I think is completely wrong. And that's part of what I'm trying to do is to show that the myth that came out of that is a myth not based on fact.

Kim And a related question is, "How is what came out of the Voyage of Discovery operative today?" What are the contemporary manifestations of it globally? This idea of expeditionary force—voyage and discovery—still resonates in foreign policy discussion today. Liz gets at that in her essay included in this collection—the discovery and the saving of people—those kinds of dialogues are still pervasive in American culture today and the fact that we are a moral nation that has God as our symbol. So you're not just colonizing for self-interested reasons, but you're colonizing because you're saving the world and you're bringing democracy to the world. She relates this still pervasive idea to the ways Lewis and Clark is celebrated today.

Craig To me, that's not what they were doing.

Kim No, not necessarily what *they* were doing, but it's the way the story is told—it's what the story means. She's saying the story means something to Americans—it's part of that overall belief system. In a way, it doesn't matter what Lewis and Clark themselves intended.

Craig Maybe we should talk about the differences between Lewis and Clark? It's kind of "the hero," singular, isn't it? Two men made into one word. To what extent do we differentiate between them?

Kim I know I didn't think about them as individuals until I read Ambrose's book that foregrounds Lewis.[5] Now I know that they were very different people and their lives had very different outcomes.

Kathryn My son, Zion, had a comment about that. He said "I think I might have committed suicide too if you had named me Meriwether. Meriwether, that's a jacked-up name!" [laughter]

Craig It is interesting, the insistence on that being basically one word when at least one side of the equation—Lewis—was a tormented being.

Lydia In the end of my piece, I wrote, "What was he thinking when he put that buffalo robe on the floor and ended up killing himself?

Kathryn I wondered that too, why did he do all of that? Almost like . . .

Lydia Like he might have had some regrets.

Kathryn Maybe that's what it was—almost like a ceremonial act. It seemed like he was trying to soothe his mind.

Craig Apparently a number of individuals from the expedition had significant difficulties. Several of them were charged with homicides after the expedition. They had problematic lives beyond the experience of the expedition. But in terms of Lewis, the Slaughter book argues that those guys had to adjust to a new way of thinking and a new way of being and basically that Clark was able to become more Indian and Lewis couldn't and that just led to his spiral downward.[6] Slaughter uses writings by Clark to show that he starts to talk like they record the Indians talked. And he wrote a speech about their horses being stolen even before they were stolen. In his journal he wrote a speech about how he was going to talk about it even though it hadn't happened yet—that in a dream he heard the horses talk to him and say they'd be taken. It's just really interesting. Because Clark *could* accommodate himself to this new way of *being* out there—he lived, whereas Lewis couldn't accommodate himself. He was too "civilized" and he couldn't accommodate himself to this other mindset.

Kathryn Do you have any historical insight as to why he committed this suicide the way that he did? Did he leave any notes?

Craig He was in debt, big time. He was supposedly mismanaging funds and he had the worst case of writer's block. He got back and he hadn't written one word. He was supposed to write up the journals because he was supposedly the best writer. And he didn't write one word from 1806-1809 despite pressure from Jefferson to publish.

Kim If you read Stephen Ambrose's *Undaunted Courage,* he makes the case that by our standards today, Lewis would probably have been considered mentally ill—bipolar disorder—although they didn't have that term then. He didn't deal as well as Clark emotionally with the trials of being immersed in other cultures and with a bunch of charges who didn't always do things the way he wanted them done.

Craig For small offenses he would go ballistic. And these are things we don't hear about. For example, a hatchet was stolen. Well, they didn't know it was stolen. A hatchet was lost and Lewis wanted to burn that Indian camp—the whole camp. The guy was almost off his rocker. I think Cruzatte tried to kill him [laughter]. I think you can make a strong argument that Cruzatte tried to kill him. The story is that Cruzatte thought Lewis was an elk and shot him, but I think he knew it was Lewis and he really *tried* to shoot him and because he only had one eye, he missed and got him in the butt! [laughter]

But before we stop, Gladys, if you feel comfortable, I'd like to hear the rest of that story about Ed Hawk. Was this along the Grand River where he lived?

Gladys That's right. In fact, the Corps built a park there—it's called Indian Camp. And people still come there—there are RV hookups there. That was part of the plan of the Corps.

Craig So the water was backing up from the Missouri River dam up the Grand River? And so they came in and they just bulldozed his house?

Gladys Yes, but he was living along the Missouri—he was at the part where the Fool Soldiers Band commemoration was, near the place they call Mile Long Bridge.

Craig So what's the fuller story on that? Why did they just come and bulldoze him?

Gladys He wasn't the only one. But he just wouldn't sign and he was in his 80s. The water was backing up and I think they just wanted him out of there because they wanted to clear that bottom land as much as they could.

Kim So if they bulldozed and you didn't sign, does that mean you didn't get any compensation at all?

Gladys I don't know that. . . But many people were instantly displaced—were made instantly homeless.

Craig What happened to Mr. Hawk? Do you know?

Gladys I know that they finally moved him into a house in town—in Wakpala [SD]. And he lived there a very short time and then of course he died. This displacement really had an effect on a whole bunch of families because whole families lived together. And now they were displaced and they could no longer live together as family units and so they had hard times. They had hard times finding places. And I kind of blame our tribe for this in part—I'm not putting the whole blame on them. They weren't educated enough to really have a big plan up there to meet the needs of these people who were suffering.

So, there was a white man from McLaughlin. His name was Wendell Keller. He moved a bunch of these one-room shacks into town and boy he was making lots of money off of that, charging rent. No running water, and of course no indoor bathrooms. So there were a lot of people coming in and making money off of these people. And so that's an impact of the flooding—a direct impact and I blame that on the river [project]. Even though for all the good that it did, we're back to square one. There's no water there. I mean there's a lake there, but we have water problems everywhere, on the reservation especially. So that's just what I experienced with my own eyes and my own knowledge during that time. So I couldn't tell you more than what I know.

Craig Do you know what happened to those two sorrel horses of Ed Hawk's?

Gladys When he moved into town, there was no place. The grazing land was gone. What could you do with them? People who had a lot of horses, who had a lot of chickens—there was no place to take them in town. There was no place where maybe they could put up a chicken coop and continue with that way of life. So, I don't know what happened. They probably sold them.

Craig Or people might have just taken them too. . .

Lydia People were self-sufficient then. They raised stock and they had gardens and then to be placed into town where they had no income, no water, and no lights. . .

Gladys You know, there was a cultural side to the loss too. My grandmother died when I was only about 11. But I lived with her during that time. And here's what I saw. When she had a hide she would take it down to the river and she would stake it on the side of the water that was flowing—for days, I don't know how many days. That was her way of cleansing that hide and stretching it out and drying it—using part of it for rawhide and the other part for tan hide—for the tops of the moccasins. So that cultural way was also taken from us. I don't know how they tan hides now. They even have classes on it: "How to tan hide." When I saw that, I thought "Oh, my God!" The way that I saw it certainly can't be what they're teaching. Because I saw it step by step by step, how she did it. If I were to tan hide, I would want a river close by so I could do it the particular way that my grandmother did. But if I were to do that today, I'd keel over because I am no longer the resourceful person that my grandmother was at 80. You see, the loss of that way of life is what the river [project] did to us.

The other thing that I've noticed is that we can no longer go by the weather and predict how we're going to prepare. I think that has a lot to do with the water and the trees. What little trees we had are no longer there. We could predict different things by the river, the trees, the birds, the animals—the way they acted.

Kim But if the river's changed and the birds and animals are gone, you have no way of knowing.

Gladys You have no way of knowing all of those things. We lived so close and we depended on these birds and animals, on how they acted, how they sang, the owls at night. Now we watch the TV and they tell us the weather forecast and that's what we're going by today. But the Indians had their own natural ways of interpreting a lot of that.

Lydia Cultural knowledge.

Craig Can that cultural knowledge—can those interpretive skills and abilities—can new ones develop along this type of a river?

Gladys Probably, but not as thorough as the way I was raised.

Lanniko So much knowledge needs to be a part of the language for you to have a conversation. We need a new language and a new knowledge of that landscape—new because the landscape has changed after the river changed. And in order to articulate our ongoing experiences, to interact, to be reflective, to listen to the small voice and the great barrenness which is our river today—we need the kind of language I'm talking about, the kind of language that's been lost to a great degree and that we need to redevelop.

Lydia It will probably take generations to develop that new conversation.

Gladys It begins in the soil. The soil has changed. For example, let's say that you want to transplant ceyaka[7] along the river. Maybe it will grow. Maybe it won't. But it all depends on that soil that's underneath. It has changed from the flooding. What did it bring? We don't know. So whether or not that will be an annual plant that grows by itself—you don't know that. You can't depend on that. Whereas when the river was there, you knew where to go to pick certain things because you knew it was there.

Craig So, in a positive long-term look, we as a people can develop that new type of relationship?

Gladys I think it's possible. We can try, I guess. There are people out there who are trying that. At Sitting Bull College, Linda Bishop-Jones teaches about native plants—ethnobotany.

Lanniko Her educational foundation is in traditional western botany. The tribal aspect of it is new to her program and our elders have been helping bring her knowledge up to where we have a compatible understanding of the landscape. She is learning the plants' stories.

Kathryn I don't think it will ever get to that again—to what Mrs. Hawk is telling us about—that we'll have all of the elements around us that can tell us how the winter's going to be, how tomorrow's going to be. My grandpa used to talk about that and I never even memorized it, how he used to ask, when the beavers build their lodges in a certain part of the lake, is it close to the shore or out in the middle? He would predict the winter by that. My grandma used to say how the day would be tomorrow by the sunset. She would say, when it goes down as a red ball like that it will be a good day—a sunny and clear day tomorrow and then you can do things outside. But I think technology interrupts that too much and I think that kind of knowledge is only going to be relegated to universities, colleges, and special interest sections of bookstores. I think that we ourselves as Native people are too interrupted by technology. It's permeated our modern, daily Indian-ness. In the TV generation you can really see the loss of our language. Up on my reservation, a lot of the cultural ways are leaving us because of that technology. It's a double-edged sword. We can watch KELO-land news and see these blizzards forming way out there and coming in—these Alberta Clippers. But if we were out on our own, especially now, without that knowledge that died with our grandparents, we'd be probably caught in a blizzard and die for our lack of knowledge.

Lydia So, are we beaten down and are we quitting? Hell no! [laughter all around]

Gladys The change in environment has also affected our stories—stories associated with the river. But now, with the way the water is, say, and twenty years down the line, are there going to be stories on that same level—of, say, Inktomi—that were associated with all of these elements of the surrounding area, the land and everything? They won't be the same and so it has affected that possibility. Let me give you an example. Inktomi stories about coyote, rabbit, and others—common stories that were native to us—were associated with all of the natural elements. They came out of the natural environment that we were familiar with. But if you take away the natural world as we knew it, you can no longer create or tell the stories. You can't tell the stories anymore to younger generations because those animals are no longer there to be used to tell the stories in order to teach the values those stories were intended to teach. And the stories don't resonate with the young people because of that.

Lydia Disrupting the river disrupted a way of life and a way of transferring knowledge. It broke a link. And it was not just the river, but also the boarding schools.

Gladys There is an absence there. The whole generation is changing. The other thing is, and I know that this is probably on all the reservations, but we are really experiencing on Standing Rock a lot of young people taking their own lives. Now we try to reason as to why. She [gesturing to Lydia] talked about that one time and she came up with some possible reasons—one of which was that children have nothing to do. Their parents are not there. We have a different way of life today where one parent is working here and the other is working over there. When the children come home from school, there is no parent there. Right away, they turn the TV on and they play these games and they see all of this drama—all of this crime. And when they have a personal problem—and everyone has problems—who are they going to turn to talk about it?

When we were growing up, we and our parents were constantly associated with the land and the river. We had something to do. We had our parents to listen to us, to tell us when to plant, how to take care of a horse. Even that by itself could be a whole class, how to take care of a horse. Now that generation today has no experience with any kind of things that make sense to them except the fact that they want to copy other kinds of generations, listen to hip-hop. They want to be noticed. There really are no black and white answers to why they take their lives. We just buried one here about two weeks ago, I think. The young man who killed himself was 16 and absolutely a nice-looking young man. Now, even his parents don't know why he did that. At his funeral—they had a huge funeral for him—they heard some younger ones saying, "Do you think that if we killed ourselves, we'd have a big funeral like this? Are they going to pay attention to us?" That's what we're hearing, because we're aggrandizing that young man through this funeral. He's actually a hero in their sight and that's a sad part of it.

Lydia The kids don't have the outlets that we had growing up. Like when we had problems, we had ceremonies. We went into a sweat to pray and talk about our problems in the sweat. And people, you know, talked to you afterwards and encouraged you. When we were kids and we went into a ceremony, everyone listened and people supported and encouraged one another, but some people don't have that anymore. The positive thing is that people are realizing what was almost lost and they are relearning and restoring what was nearly lost.

Lanniko When I was growing up, the river was not just industry to us. It gave us fuel, water, food, furniture, clothing, toys. Everything that we had came from the river—including the bullhead puppets [laughter].[8] Up the river were little dams where there were little creeks where those bullheads were. But what I was going to say was that we had not just a physical sense of who we were, but we were tired at night from the work. We would go to bed and sleep and our nights were filled with wonderful dreams of our experiences. And now we have a generation of young people who don't have such experiences—such interpretations of a world in their dreams. I wonder about that all the time. If they don't have that way of contributing to the community, by hauling wood to the elders, such things that bring value to us as a person—are they turning their knowledge of who they are—in terms of our community—inward? Do they look to see a worthless being, a person who is in the way or who is the butt of someone else's anger? If you are a young person in today's world, this is what the aftermath of the river changing has brought. There is a world of difference between understanding through knowledge of place how the world has come about and understanding the world through what these young people have—canned knowledge.

Across from the [Sacajawea Learning] center we have in Mobridge, I have watched a whole hillside slide into the river. Every time she comes over [gesturing to Gladys], we go out and look at that hill. We're going to go over there [gesturing to the group]. We need to be on that river when we're talking about it! We need to be physically standing on the river to look out across, to see the hills; the places we once played on are now silt. Who is telling the story of this devastation? It's good that we have something to say about the bicentennial commemoration, but the more important conversation is related to the ongoing legacy of scientists trying to put their imprint on the landscape—tearing up the land. And even our Indian people feel they need to engage successfully in making money off the land in order to survive. But as Indian people, we used to know and live off the resources that were there. We knew not to alter it in such a way that those resources would then not be there for us.

Kim There's one final question that should be addressed. What are your hopes for this book—why do you think it's important that we have this conversation? Why did you want to be a part of this project in the first place?

Kathryn I feel it is important to have Native voices speaking about this whole thing. It seems that many times nationally in the United States our voices are so little and do not have impact, nor are they sought. I thought that this was a good opportunity to be able to say something. And as we have said, writing is cathartic. The loss that I experienced as a child in Lower Brule—if you write about it you don't have to go out and hatchet somebody [laughter].

Lydia I feel similar to Kathryn. This is an opportunity to express ourselves— our thoughts—what we really think about that journey and how it affected all of us.

Craig I think it's a chance to write something that's contrary. It's a chance to examine the Lewis and Clark myth using the evidence. Collectively, as Oak Lake Writers, it's a wonderful opportunity to participate with published authors who are Lakota, Nakota, or Dakota. I think it's important to promote that type of literature. In terms of the book itself, it will be evident that we don't all think the same and that is a very important educational message—that is, that there isn't "the" Indian viewpoint on this. We're going to have viewpoints on the importance of Lewis and Clark and all aspects of this bicentennial commemoration.

Gladys It's an opportunity to preserve our personal experiences as we lived along the river and for readers to try to understand and to imagine how it really was when now there is nothing there to help us go back and investigate how it was.

Lanniko I have a fourteen-year-old daughter and I want her knowledge of history to be whole—not just what's in a textbook. When we look at the standard South Dakota geography book, there's no mention of what we've been discussing here and yet that is a sanctioned part of the curriculum that has been developed for all of our public schools, including the tribal schools. And that's the reason I feel that it's important to make what little contribution I can make to bringing that history that is not in any textbook.

Also, we can't really begin a conversation about Indians' role as stewards unless we talk about participating in river management. How can we get the river flowing again or help make changes that will recover the resources that were lost? We have something that non-Native people don't have. They need to be able to digest someone else's experience of the phenomenon of Mnisose before they can have a re-direction in their thinking.

Kim My reason is much the same as Craig's. First, I was thrilled when I heard about the Oak Lake Writers because I lived on both coasts for a while and grew weary of being the only Indian among other writers. I didn't want to serve the purpose people too often wanted me to serve—to have the perspectives and demeanor they expected me to have. When Liz told me about the Oak Lake Writers, I thought "Wow, I can sit around with other Dakota, Lakota and Nakota people" and that is a unique opportunity, as is being in South Dakota with other writers. Having grown up here, I always thought the great writers were in other places, but they're here too. So, I was very inspired by that.

Second, because I focus on "cultural studies," for lack of a better term, I am really interested in the cultural politics surrounding Lewis and Clark today. I'm not so much interested in who they were as individuals. What is fascinating is the way Americans are constructing an identity and using them as symbols. And so this is a chance to think about American nationalism, particularly white American nationalism. Lewis and Clark are a good vehicle for thinking about and critiquing those ideas.

NOTES
[1] A Lakota traditional chief and the keeper of the Sacred Buffalo Calf Pipe.
[2] Editors' note: Kathryn Akipa was uncomfortable mentioning in her autobiographical piece (also published in this collection) the caskets on the river. She felt that using that image might be to capitalize in her individually written piece on particularly painful memories of the desecration of the dead.

However, she was more comfortable leaving the reference in the dialogue transcript because the image was shared in conversation among L/D/Nakota people, thereby representing an exchange or mutual remembering rather than an individual promulgation.

[3] Vine Deloria Jr. and Dan Wildcat, *Power and Place: Indian Education in America* (Golden, Colorado: Fulcrum Publishing, 2001).

[4] "Little Pompy" (a nickname apparently given by Clark) is what Lanniko remembers Lakota people calling Jean-Baptiste Charbonneau, the son of Sacajawea and the Corps of Discovery interpreter, Touissant Charbonneau.

[5] Stephen E. Ambrose, *Undaunted Courage: Meriwether Lewis, Thomas Jefferson, and the Opening of the American West* (New York: Simon & Schuster, 1996).

[6] Thomas P. Slaughter, *Exploring Lewis and Clark: Reflections on Men and Wilderness* (New York: Alfred A. Knopf, 2003).

[7] Lakota word for "tobacco."

[8] Just prior to the taping of the dialogue, Lanniko Lee told the group a hilarious story from her childhood. Her uncles made puppets from the heads of bull head fish they caught in Mnisose. They dressed the puppets up in hats and made wigs for them and put on impromptu puppet shows at the dinner table.

Solitary

Kim TallBear

for Arlene Heminger Lamb

A chair in grass that turns to sand
and rocks at the river.
The rod, the flies bright painted or
nightcrawlers,
what was needed for
slow water.
She was a fisherwoman.
She had a granddaughter who stayed
cool in green rooms all day
not liking sun, breathed cream-coffee
turned cold in her grandmother's cup.
The fisherwoman sat
solitary, breathing rocks, wet
like earth, breathing sweet grass, the field.
'Cross the narrow water,
old, dry, cut boughs,
shade for the people,
the old dance grounds.
Perhaps she imagined bells jingle,
the hide of the drum, a deep voice
contest calling.
She must have felt her house
at her back, a mile up the road.
She'd wanted it so long.

A chair of island wood and fiber.
The granddaughter sits there
at the breakfast table, light dim
in the rainy season morning
beneath a whirring fan.
No grass, no rock, no rod.
No river, but the brown-silt Java Sea
beyond the teeming villages
and cities and the volatile
mountain and her hot cup of cream-
coffee in the cage of her hands.
She sits breathing, thinks of the river
or the grandmother, the green rooms
in the house in a field
in sprawling country
nearly empty
of people.
Solitary, breathing
memory.

NOTE
This poem was previously published in *South Dakota Review* and is reprinted here with permission.

Mni Wiconi

Lydia Whirlwind Soldier

Source of eternal energy
spiritual law, ancient Lakota teachings
tell us the water is wiconi
life everlasting

River Power

Lanniko L. Lee

Yes, we do know
of river power,
of love in different forms,
of comic bullheads
and waterbug adventures,
of dragon people imagined,
little people flying
over the water
in our twilight dreams
along a ghost summer
of river flowing,
shorelines lapping away,
a time passed, but not forgotten.

CONTRIBUTOR NOTES

Kathryn Akipa is a member of the Sisseton Wahpeton Oyate in South Dakota and the Heipa District. Her mother is Blossom Keeble and her grandparents were Evelyn DuMarce Crawford and Samuel Crawford. Kathryn taught at the college level for 13 years at the Southwest Polytechnic Institute and presently teaches Dakota Studies at Sisseton-Wahpeton College. She also cares for her mother. She has published her creative writing in various college newsletters and most recently in *Ikce Wicasta.*

Elizabeth Cook-Lynn, one of the writers of the twentieth-century Native American Literary renaissance, is the author of three novellas, a collection of poems, and several non-fiction works, the latest titled *Anti-Indianism is Modern America: A Voice from Tatekeya's Earth* (2001, University of Illinois Press). She is a founding editor of an academic journal, *The Wicazo Sa Review*, housed now at Arizona State University, where she is also a visiting professor in American Indian Studies. Her collection of essays, *Why I Can't Read Wallace Stegner: A Tribal Voice* (1996, University of Wisconsin Press) was awarded the Myers Center Award for the Study of Human Rights in North America in 1997. Cook-Lynn is a member of the Crow Creek Sioux Tribe, Fort Thompson, SD, and lives in the Black Hills of South Dakota.

Gladys Hawk is an enrolled member of the Standing Rock Sioux Tribe. She comes from the Hunkpapa band of the Teton Lakota. She graduated from Wakpala High School where she grew up. She received an A.A. from Sitting Bull College and her B.S. in Human Services with a minor in Indian Studies from Black Hills State College. She has a Master's degree in Tribal Leadership and Management from Oglala Lakota College. She has been a Lakota language and culture instructor for more than 30 years. She currently works at Sitting Bull College. She has also been a visiting professor at Black Hills State, an instructor at the Marty Indian School on the Yankton Reservation, and an Indian culture teacher at the Wakpala Public School. She has published an essay in *Country Congregations: South Dakota Stories.*

Craig Howe earned a Ph.D. from the University of Michigan and teaches in the Graduate Studies Department at Oglala Lakota College. He served as deputy assistant director for cultural resources at the National Museum of the American Indian, Smithsonian Institution, and director of the D'Arcy McNickle Center for American Indian History at the Newberry Library. He has developed innovative hypermedia tribal histories projects and creative museum exhibitions, taught Native studies courses in the US and Canada, and authored articles and book chapters on numerous topics, including tribal histories, Native studies, museum exhibitions and community collaborations. Howe was raised on his family's cattle ranch on the Pine Ridge Indian Reservation and is an enrolled member of the Oglala Sioux Tribe.

Lanniko L. Lee was born and raised along the Missouri River on what was formerly Armstrong County in South Dakota. She received her baccalaureate degree from Arcadia University, Glenside, Pennsylvania and a Masters of Arts degree in English from the Bread Loaf School of English, Middlebury College. She is a charter member of the Oak Lake Writers' Society. Her book reviews, articles, essays, and poetry have appeared in several publications, including *The American Indian Culture and Research Journal, Paintbrush, Ikce Wicasta, Shaping Survival, One House, Many Skies, Whole Terrain, Writer's Forum*, and *Country Congregations*. A writer, Lee has taught English and communication skills in both South Dakota public schools and state universities. Currently, Lee is an active humanities scholar and lecturer at civic and community organizations and teaches at the Sitting Bull College at Fort Yates, North Dakota and the Sacagawea Learning Center in Mobridge, South Dakota. She also owns and operates the Birdsong Inn and Guest House in Java, South Dakota.

Kim TallBear is Assistant Professor of American Indian Studies at Arizona State University in Tempe. Her research focuses on science as culture, particularly narratives of race and indigeneity in population genetics methods and research. She has published book reviews and poems in journals including the *En'owkin Journal of First North American Peoples, The South Dakota Review, The Wicazo Sá Review*, and *Xcp* (the Journal of Cross Cultural Poetics). She is a member of the Sisseton-Wahpeton Oyate in South Dakota (Big Coulee District). and is also descended from the Cheyenne and Arapaho Tribes of Oklahoma.

Elden Lawrence is a member of the Sisseton Wahpeton Oyate in South Dakota. One of 10 children, he attended the Flandreau Indian School briefly, and then enlisted in the United States Army at the age of 17, where he served six years, including a tour of duty in Korea. Having obtained his GED certificate, he then completed an undergraduate degree at Sisseton Wahpeton College, and later he earned a Ph.D in Rural Sociology from South Dakota State University. Following his graduate work, he served as President of Sisseton Wahpeton College for several years, providing leadership during an especially challenging transitional time for that institution. He also served for two terms on the Sisseton Wahpeton Oyate Tribal Council, and one term as Tribal Secretary. He is now Visiting Professor of Ethnic Studies, University of Minnesota-Mankato. His publications include a recent book, The Peace Keepers: Indian Christians and the Dakota Conflict. Elden and his wife Kim have two children, Derrick and Deborah, and six grandchildren.

Gabrielle Wynde Tateyuskanskan is an educator, speaker, visual artist, and poet who lives with her family in the rural community of Enemy Swim on the Lake Traverse Reservation. Her visual artwork is included in the permanent collections of St. Joseph School, Red Cloud School, Pierre Cultural Heritage Museum in South Dakota and private collections. Gabrielle is active in promoting social change and restorative justice through her work on the Dakota Commemorative Walk.

Joel Waters was born and raised in South Dakota. He is Oglala Sioux and is currently attending college. Some of his writings have appeared in *Red Ink* magazine, the anthology *Genocide of the Mind*, and a new anthology *Tasting Fire, Eating Blood* due out in the spring of 2006.

Lydia Whirlwind Soldier is a Sicangu Lakota born in Bad Nation on the Rosebud reservation in South Dakota. She is an enrolled member of the Rosebud Sioux Tribe. She has worked in education for thirty years. She has a Master's in Education Administration from Pennsylvania State University. Lydia is a poet, nonfiction writer, business owner and recognized craftswoman. In 1994 she received first place at the Northern Plains Tribal Arts exposition in Sioux Falls, SD, for a traditional cradleboard. Her collection of poems, *Memory Songs,* was published in 1999.

Charmaine White Face, Zumila Wobaga, is from the Oglala band of the Titonwan Oceti Sakowin. Although a political writer, her topics also include the environment, human rights, and personality profiles. Prior to writing, she taught science and math at the college level, including classes in environmental science. She resides within the confines of the Great Sioux Reservation.

Zion Zetina, "Wanbdi Hoskina", 22, is the son of Kathryn Akipa and Roberto Zetina. Zion is Sisseton Wahpeton Dakota on his mother's side and Maya/Aztec on his father's side. Zion's maternal grandmother is Dr. Blossom Keeble from the Heipa District on the Lake Traverse Reservation. His great-grandparents were Evelyn DuMarce Crawford and Samuel J. Crawford. He is a direct descendent of Wakan Inape (Charles Crawford) and Akipa. Zion has always been very conscious of and has made it a point to know the histories of his tribal affiliations. He is a grass dancer as well as a member of the Aztec dance group that his father belongs to. Much of his work is written to his generation and many of them draw inspiration from his performances. Most recently, Zion was South Dakota's 2004 Festival of the Book Slam Poetry Champion.

GLOSSARY

Akicita - Soldier or messenger.

Ceyaka - Tobacco.

Dakota - The eastern linguistic and geographic division of the Oceti Sakowin, or Sioux people. It is comprised of four nations: Mdewakantonwan, Wahpetonwan, Wahpekute and Sisitonwan.

Ihanktonwan - One of two nations of the Nakota division of the Oceti Sakowin.

Ihanktonwanna - One of two nations of the Nakota division of the Oceti Sakowin.

Inajin po - Stand up!

Inktomi - A trickster figure in Oceti Sakowin folklore. Often depicted as a coyote, inktomi literally means "spider" in Lakota.

Lakota - The western linguistic and geographic division of the Oceti Sakowin, or Sioux people. It is comprised of one nation, Titonwan.

Mdewakantonwan - One of four nations of the Dakota division of the Oceti Sakowin.

Mnisose - The Missouri River.

Mni wiconi - Water is life.

Nakota - The middle division of the Oceti Sakowin, or Sioux people. It is comprised of two nations: Ihanktonwan and Ihanktonwanna.

Oceti Sakowin - Literally translated as Seven Council Fires, this confederacy, commonly called the "Sioux," is comprised of seven major nations. Four of them are Dakotas, two are Nakotas and one is Lakota.

Paha Sapa - The Black Hills of South Dakota. Also called He Sapa.

Sisitonwan - One of four nations of the Dakota division of the Oceti Sakowin.

Titonwan - The Lakota nation of the Oceti Sakowin.

Toksta - Just wait, in time, later. (*toksa* in Lakota)

Tunkasila - Grandfather; a personal endearing name for God.

Unci Maka - Grandmother Earth.

Wahpekute - One of four nations of the Dakota division of the Oceti Sakowin.

Wahpetonwan - One of four nations of the Dakota division of the Oceti Sakowin.

Wasicu - Anglo-Americans. The Literal definition of this word is usually given as either "persons who are mysterious or sacred" or as "persons who take the fat of meat."

Wakan Tanka - Great Mystery or Great Sacredness (as in a sacred quality too great to understand with the finite mind); God.

Wokiksuye - To remember.

ADDITIONAL READINGS

Ambrose, Stephen. (1996). *Undaunted Courage: Meriwether Lewis, Thomas Jefferson, and the Opening of the American West.* New York: Simon & Schuster, 1996.

A widely heralded, easily accessible narrative of the Lewis and Clark expedition, *Undaunted Courage* created a ground swell of interest in the bicentennial of the expedition and was the basis for the PBS film by Ken Burns.

Buechel, Eugene. (1983). *Dictionary of Teton Sioux.* Pine Ridge, SD: Red Cloud Indian School, 1983.

An authoritative dictionary complied by a German Jesuit who lived on the Rosebud Reservation around the turn of the 20th Century.

Burns, Ken. (1997). *Lewis & Clark: The Journey of the Corps of Discovery.* The American Lives Film Project. Burbank, CA: PBS Home Video.

A popular film based on the book *Undaunted Courage* by Stephen Ambrose, who also appears in many scenes.

Ronda, James. (1984). Lewis and Clark Among the Indians. Lincoln: University of Nebraska Press.

One of the few books that attempts to examine Indian perspectives of the expedition by contextualizing the journals of Lewis and Clark with ethnographic information.

Library of Congress. [memory.loc.gov/learn/features/lewisandclark/index.html]

This Library of Congress website is content-rich with extensive links to materials within and beyond the LC.

Moulton, Gary (Ed.). *The Definitive Journals of Lewis & Clark: From the Ohio to the Vermillion,* Vol. 2 (1986), *Up the Missouri to Fort Mandan,* Vol. 3 (1987), and Over the Rockies to St. Louis, Vol. 8 (1993). Lincoln: University of Nebraska Press.

Available in paperback, these three volumes of a five-volume set present the journals of Lewis and Clark covering the time the expedition was in Oceti Sakowin country, both on its trip up the Missouri in 1804 and its rapid descent in 1806.

Moulton, Gary (Ed.) T*he Definitive Journals of Lewis & Clark: The Journal of John Ordway*, Vol. 9 (1996), *The Journal of Patrick Gass*, Vol. 10 (1996), and *The Journals of Joseph Whitehouse*, May 14, 1804-April 2, 1806, Vol. 11 (1997). Lincoln: University of Nebraska Press.

Three volumes of the 13-volume set in which Moulton re-edits the previously published journals of the three expedition sergeants. These are the only known first-hand written accounts, other than those of Lewis and Clark, by expedition members.

National Geographic. (2000). *Lewis & Clark: Great Journey West*. Burbank, CA: National Geographic Television.

A detailed reenactment of the journey shot on-location. Originally in IMAX format, the DVD version was released in 2002 and includes many extras, including an interactive map.

Slaughter, Thomas. (2003). *Exploring Lewis and Clark: Reflections on Men and Wilderness*. New York: Alfred A. Knopf.

An interesting, and sometimes far-reaching, analysis of the psychological impact on the two captains of the new lands and peoples the expedition encountered.